Western Movies

Western Movies

Edited by **William T. Pilkington**
and **Don Graham**

Illustrations by **Laura Butler**

UNIVERSITY OF NEW MEXICO PRESS

Albuquerque

Library of Congress Cataloging in Publication Data

Main entry under title:

Western movies.

   Bibliography: p. 156
   CONTENTS: Pilkington, W. T. and Graham. D.   Intro-
duction, a fistful of westerns.—Trimmer, J. F. The
Virginian (1929 and 1946).—Clandfield, D. Stage-
coach (1939).—Pilkington, W. T. Fort Apache (1948).
—Graham, D. High Noon (1952).—Folsom, J. K. Shane
(1953) and Hud (1963). [etc.]
   1. Western films—History and criticism—Addresses,
essays, lectures,   I. Pilkington, William T.
II. Graham, Don, 1940–
PN 1995.9.W4W38   791.43′0909′32   78-21427
ISBN 0-8263-0496-6   ISBN 0-8263-0497-4 [Pbk.]

PN
1995
.9
.W4
.W38

To Michael
and
To Sheila and Vicky

Acknowledgments

We wish to express our gratitude to the following people: Carol Carey, of the Stills Archive of the Museum of Modern Art, for assistance in locating appropriate illustrations; Jack Nachbar and Michael Marsden, of Bowling Green State University, for much helpful advice; Laura Butler, of Mingus, Texas, for her excellent drawings; and Beth Hadas, of the University of New Mexico Press, for encouragement and expert editorial help.

Backward, turn backward, film guy, in your flight,
And turn out a cowboy that does the game right.
Put on a picture that won't look so strange
To us old punchers who've rode on the range.
                    —from John A. Lomax and Alan Lomax, *Cowboy*
                              Songs and Other Frontier Ballads (1948)

North of Tel Aviv, the set of an old Western town built
to film a number of low-budget European-made films a few
years back sits empty, awaiting the return of the cowboy
movie.
          —from a news story in the Austin, Texas, *American-Statesman,*
                                              August 24, 1978

Contents

1

INTRODUCTION: A FISTFUL OF WESTERNS

William T. Pilkington and Don Graham

Several years ago a reviewer for the *New York Times* condescendingly referred to Western movies as "that peculiar genre."[1] If we understand *peculiar* to mean (as the dictionary defines the term) "unlike anything else or anything of the same class or kind," then Westerns are without question peculiar. Westerns are America's unique contribution to that body of mythic lore familiar to most of the human race. They embrace a cycle of stories and character types as rich and fascinating and as susceptible of near-infinite variation as the medieval tales of King Arthur and his knights. The Western film genre, writes George N. Fenin, makes "a universal appeal to the universal imagination. It is the only aspect of the American cinema that is readily understood in Rome, Moscow, Tokyo, Bangkok, Sydney, Cairo, and Buenos Aires."[2]

Another way of saying this is that Westerns function as epics: they translate national experience into popular images. John Wayne has spoken eloquently to this point, commenting in a recent television interview on the kinship between Westerns and Homeric epics. Both, he said, focus on the essentials in human nature and experience. John Wayne is not the only observer to liken Westerns to Greek epics. André Bazin, the famous French critic, writing in the early 1950s, placed the Western in the "epic category" because of its heroes, recurring legends, and simple but necessary morality.[3]

The epic qualities and symbolic content of Westerns thus remain a strong referential touchstone in American culture. Why else

---

1

would a recent cover of *Esquire* magazine (March 1, 1978) present such a familiar icon from Western movies: a lawman dressed in formal-looking, dark pinstripes, striding alone down an empty street, his badge pinned on his breast, his face lined with stoic fortitude. The lawman was, of course, Gary Cooper; the movie, *High Noon*. Even Americans who had not seen the movie could identify the figure; it possesses the subliminal cognitive impact of myth. The story for which the cover was designed dealt with individuals who had singlehandedly taken on powerful corporations; these were tales of legal machinations, corporate power plays, white-collar injustice, far removed in time, setting, and complexity from the world of *High Noon*. Yet the editor's strategy of using Gary Cooper to symbolize the plight of individualism in the 1970s, a quarter-century after the movie and seventy-odd years after the end of the historical epoch dramatized in the movie, well expresses the double-edged and lasting power of Western movies.

From the beginning, Westerns have been a staple product of the motion picture industry. Though the record is cloudy on this point, it is generally believed that the first American movie to feature an original narrrative storyline was Edwin S. Porter's ten-minute Western, *The Great Train Robbery* (1903). Filmed "on location" in the wilds of New Jersey, it was the first of many Westerns made on the East Coast before the industry—for reasons of climate, scenery, and economy—shifted its headquarters to California. Throughout the twentieth century Westerns have endured as a significant and profitable part of the movie business. They have done so in part because of the genre's remarkable pliancy: it has always been able to change to meet changing attitudes and social conditions.

Yet Westerns, as a movie type, have seemed continually on the brink of extinction; the genre has effected more improbable escapes from peril than the legendary Pauline. In the early days—when dozens of "B" Westerns were made every year—many critics deplored the low artistic quality of the films and warned of their dire effects on the young, dismissing the form as an anachronistic and puerile subgenre that no thinking adult could possibly take seriously. Even today, such critics as John Simon, themselves anachronistic moralists, refuse to consider the Western as anything but, as Simon says, an "infantile genre" preoccupied with the "wrong values."[4] Such lofty disdain has rarely if ever altered the course of popular entertainment; the Western survived its early detractors, just as it will survive John Simon.

From the 1920s to the 1950s the Western enjoyed extraordinary popularity among generations of young people who inhabited movie houses on Saturday mornings and afternoons, thrilling to the exploits of Tom Mix, Ken Maynard, Hoot Gibson, Gene Autry, Roy Rogers, William Boyd, and many another courageous cowboy star. Admittedly most of the Westerns that featured these actors shamelessly exaggerated, distorted, and romanticized to the point that the reality of the old West was virtually obscured from view. Apparently, though, such movies gave audiences during those troubled times exactly what they were looking for: fantasy, escape, and a consoling interpretation of America's past. The collapse of the big-studio system spelled the end of the "B" Western. Television, rising production costs, changing tastes, and other factors altered Hollywood and, with it, the number and nature of the Westerns produced.

The appearance, in 1939, of John Ford's immensely popular *Stagecoach* was a significant event in the genre's development, since it rescued the Western from the "B"-picture category and supplied it with a new respectability. During the 1940s a series of Ford Westerns, along with the release of such highly regarded films as William Wellman's *The Ox-Bow Incident* (1943) and Howard Hawks's *Red River* (1948), further enhanced that respectability. In 1954 Robert Warshow, in a celebrated pronouncement, stated that "the possibilities of fruitful variation in the Western movie are limited," and he seemed to suggest that these possibilities were already, by the mid-1950s, nearly exhausted.[5] The early 1950s, of course, had produced a spate of classic "adult Westerns": *The Gunfighter* (1950), *High Noon* (1952), and *Shane* (1953). It is perhaps easy to understand why Warshow might have concluded that a stage had been reached beyond which it was not possible for the Western to progress. But within a couple of years after his prophecy, important contributions to the genre were made by such notable directors as Anthony Mann, Budd Boetticher, and Arthur Penn.

Far from dying, Westerns continued to thrive during the two decades following Warshow's forecast. Philip French, a leading critic of Western films, claims that the early 1970s were "one of the great periods of the genre," certainly as important to its development as the early 1950s.[6] Westerns managed to survive because they proved capable of "fruitful variation" in ways unforeseen even by so intelligent a commentator as Warshow. As audiences changed, so did the Western. In the 1960s Americans generally became more skeptical and presumably more sophisticated; they began to question the received and familiar versions of national experience. In the early sixties two kinds of heroes came to dominate the Western genre. The first, represented in such films as *Lonely Are the Brave, The Man Who Shot Liberty Valance,* and *Ride the High Country* (all released in 1962), was an anachronistic and doomed figure, often an aging cowboy who had lived beyond his time into a new, inimical era. All that remained for such heroes was a ritualistic and often unsung reenactment of the old values in a barren time. The second was a different hero altogether, an antihero. He might be something of a heel, like Paul Newman's Hud or, from the next decade, a comic survivor, one of us, like Dustin Hoffman's Jack Crabb. A particularly powerful version of the antihero found its prime expression in the greed, cynicism, and unremitting violence of Sergio Leone's mid-sixties recipe for the "spaghetti Western," a recipe that yielded some memorable concoctions: *A Fistful of Dollars, For a Few Dollars More,* and *The Good, the Bad and the Ugly.* In the late 1960s and early 1970s, so-called anti-Westerns, films that negated the simplistic verities of the myth, became increasingly popular. Such notable movies of the period as *The Wild Bunch* (1969), *Butch Cassidy and the Sundance Kid* (1969), *Little Big Man* (1970), *McCabe and Mrs. Miller* (1971), and *The Great Northfield Minnesota Raid* (1972) all, in one way or another and with more or less subtlety and cogency, turned the Western myth on its ear. A more obvious assault was carried out in comic Westerns, spoofs such as *Cat Ballou* (1964) and *Blazing Saddles* (1974) that mocked both the genre and its legacy of implicit idealism. Recent Westerns, then, to stay in tune with the times, have voiced many discouraging words—words certainly not heard in *Stagecoach* or *Red River.*

Now, once again—in the late 1970s—the genre appears to have been herded into a box canyon and has no place to go. Public opinion polls tell us that most youngsters no longer admire cowboys and few even bother to fantasize about being cowboys. Books appear with titles like *The Last Cowboy* and *The Last Cattle Drive.* Western series, with the exception of occasional reruns, have all but disappeared from American television screens. Each year fewer Western movies are produced. The Western, in the visual arts at least, seems to be dead. That, at any rate, is the conclusion of the doomsayers. But is it dead? Making gloomy predictions about a genre that has demonstrated such resilience and adaptability as has the Western over three-quarters of a century is hardly a safe occupation. Even as we write, at least two big-budget Westerns are in production: *I, Tom Horn,* starring Steve McQueen, and *Butch and Sundance: The Early Days.* Further, there is no reason to believe that such stars as Clint Eastwood, Robert Redford, Burt Lancaster, and Kirk Douglas—or even the seemingly indestructible John Wayne—have made their last Western. But whatever happens in years to come, the Western has shown itself to be, historically, American film's most popular and durable form. Rather than attempting to peer into an uncertain future, fans of the Western can, therefore, find much comfort in surveying the glories of the past.

This gathering of essays is offered as such a survey. The dozen pieces focus on a fistful of Western movies, ranging chronologically from the 1929 version of *The Virginian* to *The Missouri Breaks,* released in 1976. One critic, Jon Tuska, claims to have seen 8,000 Westerns, an experience that effected, he says, "no appreciable change in my personality or temperament. . . . My moral convictions—or utter lack of them—remain unassailed."[7] However, most people, even students of the Western, have neither the time nor the inclination to duplicate—or to come close to duplicating—Tuska's mind-boggling feat. A more selective approach seems in order. That, in any event, is the premise from which this collection of essays proceeds. The fourteen movies that are the subjects of the essays do not, we believe, require extended justification. Each film discussed is, in some sense, a landmark within the genre—a classic or near-classic or, in a few cases, an interesting failure. It may be useful first, though, before we move on to analyses of individual films, to sketch the backgrounds of critical thinking about Westerns and then to examine briefly the critical vantage points from which the authors of the essays view their subjects.

Serious critical scrutiny of Western films dates from the 1950s—specifically from the unexpected interest in the genre shown by several influential foreign critics (such as André Bazin and Jean-Louis Rieupeyrout). Since that time articles and books about Westerns have accumulated rapidly, so that today there exists a large and varied body of criticism (the Selected Bibliography at the close of this volume suggests the dimensions of that body of criticism). Some of the commentary is profound, some of it silly, but almost none of it is dull. Some of it is also delightfully wacky.

Here are a couple of our favorite examples, both drawn from somber academic journals. The first was written by a French observer in the early 1960s.[8] Following a series of cogent remarks on parallels between Westerns and European national epics, the author then set out to classify the major character types in Westerns. He settled on three categories: the bastard, the s.o.b., and the dirty rat. The bastard, it turns out, is the familiar white-hat hero; the s.o.b. is the villain; and the dirty rat, a term doubtless imported from Cagney gangster movies, is a sheriff gone weak. Our second example also stems from a crucial—and comic—misunderstanding of American idiom. The author, an M.D., hoped to analyze the psychological implications of Westerns, a form of criticism that has produced numerous attempts to explain the symbolic Freudian implications of the genre. In pursuit of the sexual meanings of guns, a favorite target of this school, the author explored the nuances of certain stock phrases for killing in Westerns: "drilling," "bumping off," and "knocking off." The last phrase led to this illumination: "The expression to knock up, means to arouse by knocking; in English colloquialism, it means to tire out or fatigue; in English slang it means to have intercourse (tire out or fatigue a woman)."[9]

Humor aside, such essays are characterized by a tendency that also appears in more searching examinations of Westerns—the tendency to minimize the richness of particular works in order to define *the* Western. The result is sometimes a provocative thesis, but when the thesis is allowed to harden into dogma, so that Westerns become only *one* kind, then the sense of multifarious possibilities is lost. Robert Warshow, a brilliant critic, illustrates the tendency in his famous essay "Movie Chronicle: The Westerner," when he announces that "the true theme of the Western movie is not the freedom and expansiveness of frontier life, but its limitations, its material baseness, the pressures of obligation."[10] Given this view, it is not surprising that Warshow prefers *The Gunfighter*, grim, realistic, tragic, to *Stagecoach*, expansive, positive, romantic. Today few critics would agree with his preference, and anybody who wants to know what the Western is certainly should be conversant with the radically different styles of *both* these benchmark movies. In effect Warshow's prescriptive statement limits the actual variety of the genre. Our point is different: there are multiple Western traditions. Thus we do not subscribe to the commonplace of "Seen one Western, seen 'em all," a notion that, curiously, unites both viewers who look down on Westerns and serious critics who want to capture once and for all the essence of *the* Western.

Three kinds of criticism seem especially to generate all-encompassing (and often reductive) theses: aesthetic, psychological, and thematic. The first of these is heavily judgmental: one movie is good, another is bad, and so forth, and often the reasons for making such judgments seem purely personal. The second kind is frequently reductive because it seeks to put movies on a couch. Such criticism can become obsessive in identifying the horse as true love object, the gun as phallus, and so on. The third kind, though, has produced some of the seminal explanations of both the content and appeal of Westerns.

The foundation for the main lines of thematic criticism was laid ten years before the first Western movie was made, in Frederick Jackson Turner's far-reaching essay of 1893, "The Significance of the Frontier in American History." Turner held that the frontier, the West, represented the real America and that it was there that individualism, democracy, and nationalism were best nourished. In Turner's intellectual scenario the frontier was "the outer edge of the wave—the meeting point between savagery and civilization."[11] This terrain is precisely where many Western movies begin. They develop their tension, their meanings, from the interaction of two kingdoms of force—civilization and savagery. In this dialectic, then, first defined abstractly by Turner, and later expanded by such important critics as John G. Cawelti, lay the particular animus of many Westerns.

The opposition of civilization and savagery seems to underlie other formulations of thematic criticism, though the sets of opposing terms bear different headings: the garden versus the wilderness, East versus West. Jim Kitses's *Horizons West* contains a useful chart (reproduced below in David Clandfield's essay on *Stagecoach*) of paired opposites, including, for example, America versus Europe, nature versus culture, freedom versus order, that clarify the dialectic tensions generated in many Westerns.[12] In still other major formulations, a similar pattern of opposites appears. Thus in the interpretation that insists upon the Western as a modern version of the morality play, the dialectic is predictably good (restraint) versus evil (license).[13] Finally, in the most recent major theory that has been advanced, the Western is seen as a symbolic vehicle for reflecting American economic ideology.[14]

Here the clash is between opposing economic forces: individual-
istic free-market capitalism versus corporate-controlled power
blocs. Such a bald statement of a complex thesis is not meant to
denigrate the theory, but simply to suggest that once again the
dialectic of opposing forces is identified as the source of energy in
Westerns. This brief survey overlooks the richness and fullness with
which each of the theories is presented by its exponents, but it will,
we hope, provide readers with possibilities for further investigation.

The essays that follow are devoted to individual films, not to
general theories. They were chosen in part as worthwhile analyses
of a range of important Western films; in part to provide a cross
section of some of the more common critical approaches to
Western movies. By way of clarifying the latter purpose, we offer
here a brief explanatory listing (by no means definitive) of some
conceptual assumptions that frequently govern the efforts of
Western film critics.

The "auteur" approach. Auteur criticism is founded on the belief
that a film's director (or, less often, the screenwriter, occasionally a
combination of the two) is the auteur, author, the shaping
intelligence that stamps a motion picture with a distinctive style
and vision of life. The concept was developed by French cinema
critics in the 1950s, particularly François Truffaut. Auteur critics
often concern themselves with ranking directors and establishing
hierarchies. The most prominent American auteur critic is Andrew
Sarris, who a decade ago drew up a list of "Pantheon Directors."[15]
Detractors of the Western genre might well ponder the fact that on
the list are John Ford and Howard Hawks—directors best known for
their Westerns. It may be shocking to some that Ford and Hawks
look down from their lofty perch alongside such worthies as D. W.
Griffith, Sergei Eisenstein, Jean Renoir, and Luis Buñuel. French
auteur critics of the 1950s also thought highly of Ford and Hawks
and of the Western as a movie type. For obvious reasons critics of
this persuasion normally explore a director's entire filmography;
when they isolate particular movies, they attempt, according to
Sarris, "to perceive in individual works the organic unity of a
director's career."[16] Of the pieces included here, William T.
Pilkington's essay on Ford, Robin Wood's on Hawks, Arthur G.
Pettit's on Sam Peckinpah, and Floyd B. Lawrence's on the Arthur
Penn–Thomas McGuane collaboration in the making of *The
Missouri Breaks* owe much to the auteur approach.

The "Western as history" approach. A Western, according to this critical view, ought to be judged on the basis of how historically accurate it is, how "realistic" and plausible its plot and characterizations are—even how authentic it is in its use of speech, clothing styles, architecture, and other background details. From this perspective a critic may choose to condemn (and they have been so condemned) "singing Westerns" of the Autry-Rogers ilk for their gross violations of the principle of verisimilitude. Needless to say, the "Western as history" theory is widely invoked in commentary on Western movies. Carried too far, though, it seems a rather elementary and misguided method for evaluating Westerns, which have ordinarily been about a bygone era—that is, as Jim Kitses puts it, they are about "an ambiguous, mercurial concept: the idea of the West."[17] In the Western the way it really was in the old West is not nearly so important as the way twentieth century audiences *think* it was. The dangers of the "Western as history" approach having been duly noted, we recommend Dan Georgakas's intelligent comments on the portrayal of Indians in *A Man Called Horse* as a model of how this theory may be usefully employed in film criticism.

The "Western as myth" approach. Criticism in this vein examines Westerns according to their relation to the "Western myth." Some kind of definition of the myth—including consideration of plot formulas, character types (the "Western hero," for example), and stock situations, symbols, and images often associated with the myth—is usually stated or implied in the critical analysis. Once a definition is established (or assumed), a particular Western may be seen as resting somewhere on the spectrum that stretches from total acceptance to total negation of the myth. *Stagecoach,* for example, is generally viewed as the archetypal Western because of its wholehearted endorsement of the myth, while a number of recent films, as mentioned earlier, come pretty close to being wholesale denials of the myth. Several of the essays below—Joseph Trimmer on *The Virginian,* David Clandfield on *Stagecoach,* Robin Wood on *Rio Bravo,* Arthur G. Pettit on *The Wild Bunch,* and Jack Nachbar on *Ulzana's Raid*—are greatly indebted to this mode of criticism.

The "literature into film" approach. The plots of many Western movies have their origins in works of literature; *The Virginian, Shane, Hud,* and *Little Big Man* are relevant instances. Comparative studies of literary works and their film adaptations can sometimes provide helpful insights into the nature of two very different media. The best studies of this sort are not content merely to point out differences in literary and movie treatments of the same story line (such differences ought to be expected and therefore assumed). Instead, they speculate on what those differences tell us about the essential qualities and conditions of the two media. Trimmer's piece on *The Virginian,* Clandfield's on *Stagecoach,* James K. Folsom's on *Shane* and *Hud,* and John W. Turner's on *Little Big Man* are all enlightening examples of this critical approach.

The "Western as allegory" approach. Westerns are the most allegorical of movie genres. Within an anachronistic chronological setting and bound by an array of conventions almost as fixed and necessary as those of pastoral poetry, the Western often comments indirectly on the political and social events of the age in which it was made. While the conventions of the genre are, in some ways, rigid and confining, they seem to allow, paradoxically, for great allegorical flexibility. Those conventions no more stifle creativity in the director of Westerns than the centuries-old forms of pastoral throttled the genius of John Milton, who in "Lycidas," a pastoral elegy, gave the world a timeless literary masterpiece. The propensity of directors and screenwriters to use the Western as a vehicle for allegory can scarcely be doubted. For instance, in the late 1960s and early 1970s many Westerns—*The Wild Bunch* and *Ulzana's Raid* have been interpreted in this way—were not about the old West at all; they were really about the American involvement in Vietnam. An interesting and even more current example is *Posse* (1975), a "Watergate Western" in which Kirk Douglas portrays a Texas sheriff whose excessive political ambitions lead to a fate very similar to that which befell a recent president. These three movies are all excellent films; they may be viewed and enjoyed with no knowledge of the topical allegory embedded in them. For some moviegoers, however, allegory supplies an added and often pleasurable dimension to the aesthetic experience of seeing a film. Don Graham's piece on *High Noon* offers a number of helpful observations on the advantages and occasional hazards of using the Western for allegorical purposes.

The "decades" approach. The "decades" theory (related in a way to the "Western as allegory" approach) assumes that many Westerns reflect the attitudes, beliefs, concerns, and deepest desires of the era (for convenience, read *decade*) in which they were made.

This approach works best in comparing different versions of the same story produced in different decades. It is also useful in contrasting the various film "biographies" of the life of some legendary figure: Billy the Kid, Jesse James. Wyatt Earp, Col. George Custer, and Belle Starr are a few examples of historical personages whose lives have been subjected to multiple cinematic treatments. Thus a movie about Billy the Kid filmed in the 1930s—a decade of economic depression and unrest—would presumably give a very different view of the Kid from one made in the early 1970s—a time of vastly altered political and social concerns. Trimmer's essay on the two versions of *The Virginian* and Graham's on *The Great Northfield Minnesota Raid* make extensive use of this critical concept.

The "structuralist" approach. Potentially, of course, almost any critical stance—formalist, feminist, moralist, Marxist, or whatever—may be assumed in examining Western movies, or for that matter any work of art or congeries of works of art. One critical theory that has lately been very much in vogue is that of structuralism. Structural analysis—which has been applied to the study of such phenomena as language, myth, literature, and culture (popular and otherwise)—attempts to discern the underlying and governing structural configuration of a given discrete entity. Not surprisingly, the principles of structuralism have framed a number of recent critical pronouncments on the Western.[18] Many critics of Westerns, Philip French observes, now "find it fruitful to operate at a point where the apparatus of Lévi-Strauss and Company of Paris impinges upon the apparel of Levi Strauss and Co. of San Francisco."[19] The results of that impingement are interesting, if hardly definitive. Clandfield's structural analysis of the microcosmic society inside John Ford's stagecoach is an excellent example of the structuralist approach; also Turner's comments on *Little Big Man* rely heavily on a basic structuralist concept.

The "genre" approach. It is no accident that this brief listing of critical approaches to the Western begins with the auteur theory and ends with the genre theory. These, it seems to us, are the polar opposites within which the other critical theories range. The auteur critic starts with the artist, with the act of creation, and examines the various aspects of a film (including, perhaps, what the auteur does with the genre he chooses to work within) from that vantage point. Conversely the genre critic begins with a model of a given form and tends to view the elements of a movie (such as the role of the director) on the basis of how those elements—and the film as a whole—relate to the form. In *American Film Genres,* Stuart M. Kaminsky says the following:

> Genre study in film is based on the realization that certain popular narrative forms have both cultural and universal roots, that the Western today is related both to archetypes of the past 200 years in the United States and to the folk tale, and the myth. . . . the genre approach makes no qualitative judgment. It is an examination of popular forms, an attempt to understand, not to "sell" films or directors.[20]

In genre analysis all films are of equal interest. Thus *Billy the Kid vs. Dracula* (c. 1966) is potentially as significant to the genre critic as, say, Arthur Penn's *The Left-Handed Gun* (1958). Obviously the genre approach overlaps several other approaches that we have discussed. It differs from the others, however, in that it encourages the critic to explore an individual motion picture in the broadest possible generic context and to show how the film enlarges and alters the form or type to which it properly belongs. Almost all the essays reprinted here employ, to one degree or another, the genre approach; one could scarcely consider the Western without dealing, if only indirectly, with the question of genre. Graham's discussion of *High Noon* and Nachbar's of *Ulzana's Raid* seem especially good illustrations of this critical mode.

The films analyzed in the following essays will come as no surprise to fans of the Western. But any Western movie buff is likely to spot some significant omissions, films that the aficionado regards as classic, pictures that he recalls with affection. We are familiar with the problem, because for various reasons not every movie that we would like to have included has been included. A particular difficulty that should be mentioned is that for a number of major Westerns there are simply no sustained critical discussions. *Red River* is an outstanding example, but there are others. Indeed when we undertook this project, we soon came to appreciate the accuracy of Jack Nachbar's observation that one area in Western film criticism needing further attention is detailed analyses of individual Westerns.[21] This collection, we hope, speaks at least in part to that need.

NOTES

1. Renata Adler, "The Screen: Zane Grey Meets the Marquis de Sade," *New York Times*, January 25, 1968, p. 33.

2. George N. Fenin, "Conclusion," in George N. Fenin and William K. Everson, *The Western: From Silents to the Seventies* (New York: Grossman Publishers, 1973), p. 379.

3. André Bazin, *What Is Cinema?* vol. 2, trans. Hugh Gray (Berkeley: University of California Press), p. 147.

4. "Academy Awards of All Time," *Saturday Evening Post* 250 (July–August 1978): 42.

5. Robert Warshow, "Movie Chronicle: The Westerner," in Robert Warshow, *The Immediate Experience* (New York: Atheneum, 1970), p. 151.

6. Philip French, *Westerns: Aspects of a Movie Genre*, rev. ed. (New York: Oxford University Press, 1977), p. 170.

7. Jon Tuska, *The Filming of the West* (Garden City, New York: Doubleday, 1976), p. xviii.

8. Rémy G. Saisselin, "Poetics of the Western," *British Journal of Aesthetics* 2 (1962): 159–169.

9. Kenneth J. Munden, "A Contribution to the Psychological Understanding of the Origin of the Cowboy and His Myth," *American Image* 15 (Summer 1958): 135.

10. Warshow, p. 144.

11. Frederick Jackson Turner, *The Significance of the Frontier in American History*, ed. Harold P. Simonson (New York: Frederick Ungar, 1976), p. 28.

12. Jim Kitses, *Horizons West* (Bloomington: Indiana University Press, 1969), p. 11.

13. For a useful discussion of the good-versus-evil pattern, see Peter Homans, "Puritanism Revisited: An Analysis of the Contemporary Screen-Image Western," *Studies in Public Communication*, Summer 1961, pp. 73–84.

14. Will Wright, *Sixguns and Society: A Structural Study of the Western* (Berkeley: University of California Press, 1975). The heart of Wright's argument appears on pp. 173–184.

15. Andrew Sarris, "Notes on the Auteur Theory in 1962," in *Film Theory and Criticism*, eds. Gerald Mast and Marshall Cohen (New York: Oxford University Press, 1974), p. 514. Andrew Sarris, *The American Cinema* (New York: E. P. Dutton, 1968), provides extensive rankings of American directors.

16. Sarris, "Notes on the Auteur Theory in 1962," p. 500.

17. Kitses, p. 8.

18. For an especially lucid discussion of how structuralism relates to the study of mass culture—though not specifically the Western—see G. R. Kress's "Structuralism and Popular Culture," in *Approaches to Popular Culture* (Bowling Green, Ohio: Popular Press, 1976), pp. 85–106.

19. French, p. 10.

20. Stuart M. Kaminsky, *American Film Genres* (New York: Dell Publishing Company, 1974), pp. 12–13.

21. Jack Nachbar, *Western Films: An Annotated Critical Bibliography* (New York: Garland Publishing Company, 1975), p. 3.

2

THE VIRGINIAN
(1929 and 1946)

Joseph F. Trimmer

*Joseph F. Trimmer is professor of English at Ball State
University, Muncie, Indiana.*

To paraphrase André Bazin, the Western is America's Odyssey.[1]
It is an epic tale of heroic men who live in the timeless world of
myth. The Western is also America's myth because it embodies all
the aspirations of our national character. It is, after all, the story of
a common man who works at a rather menial job; but in the pale
half-light of romance, the cowboy can be seen as the equal of
Achilles or Roland—the embattled knight defending his code of
gallant honor and manly virtue. And like Odysseus, we never seem
to tire of hearing our story. It was Owen Wister's *The Virginian*
which gave classic formulation to that story. Over the years the
novel has enjoyed an incredible popularity; and that popularity has
been increased by two adaptations for the screen.[2] What is
interesting in all this retelling of the same story is the significant
alterations from the original evident in each successive version. It is
not surprising or necessarily disturbing to learn that Hollywood has
not "followed the book." What is surprising is the way in which this
alteration documents significant changes in the character of the
Western myth and our attitude toward it.

One possible explanation for these changes in the character of

Joseph F. Trimmer, *"The Virginian:* Novel and Films," *Illinois Quarterly* 35 (December
1972). © 1972 by *Illinois Quarterly.* Reprinted by permission of the publisher and author.

the Virginian story is that most of them were implicit in the symbolic content of the novel. The simplest way to read Wister's novel is to see it as a novel of East and West: Wister tested the code of the Western hero by placing it in opposition to the code of Eastern civilization as represented by the schoolmarm, Molly Wood. The sexual-cultural clash which results produces a novel of mutual education for the two protagonists. Robert Warshow has argued that "in the American mind, refinement, virtue, civilization, Christianity itself, are seen as feminine and therefore women are portrayed as possessing some kind of deeper wisdom, while men, for all their apparent self-assurance, are fundamentally childish."[3] This attitude is apparent throughout the early portion of the novel as the Virginian is shown to be rather wild and given to practical joking. There is, to be sure, much of the romantic primitive in this initial portrait; the Virginian is free, content and in harmony with his environment.

But we are also aware of the Virginian's potential for education into another kind of life. There is, after all, his name, which not only indicates his origin, but his capacity to apprehend the refinement of "civilization." When the school teacher arrives in town, the Virginian becomes an admirer of Eastern culture; and with her guidance, he reads Shakespeare, Browning, Austen and Scott. Such an education makes him eventually worthy of the lady from the East. Their three-year courtship is, in fact, a model of Victorian propriety. When they finally return East after their wedding trip, the Virginian is acknowledged as a perfect gentleman by the Vermont social set.

While the Virginian is learning about Eastern culture, Molly is being educated as to the nature of the Western experience. Western civilization is primarily a masculine world—a country where men are men. In this kind of world it is the woman who is childish unless she can develop a sense of quasi-masculine independence and an understanding of the necessity of violence. In the two crisis situations of the novel, the Virginian must make ethical choices that produce moral revulsion in Molly. Molly believes in law and order and cannot understand why it is necessary to break the law in order to preserve the law. Eventually she is able to acknowledge the expedient necessity of the hanging of Steve—it was for the public good. But the second moral crisis is more difficult since it involves no obvious social benefit. On their wedding day, the Virginian and Molly quarrel over whether he shall answer or evade the challenge of Trampas. What is he fighting for, she asks. "What he defends, at bottom, is the purity of his own image—in fact his honor."[4] And the concept of honor is ironically a virtue associated with the Eastern aristocratic concept of the gentleman. As Warshow suggests, "the Westerner is the last gentleman."[5]

What we have in *The Virginian* is a reassessment of the relationship of East and West. Molly left the East and her rather prudishly cultured admirer because she was looking for a wider world of experience. The West and more particularly the Virginian gives her a wider and a revitalized picture of herself. Molly is not alone in sensing that there are deficiencies in her Eastern world. Her great aunt had the opportunity for a similar romantic adventure in her youth. She is therefore capable of recognizing the value and meaning of the Virginian. When she reads his letter of proposal, she responds by saying, "O dear, O dear! And this is what I lost."

What is accomplished in this reassessment of the relationship of East and West is a synthesis of American traditions. Donald Davis has talked about *The Virginian* as a combination of the Western scout of Cooper and the Dime Novel, and a "recasting of the golden myth of the antebellum South."[6] Donald E. Houghton sees the novel as portraying the myth of the romantic primitive, and the economic myth of Horatio Alger.[7] Houghton makes his case even more convincing by showing how the two myths are given separate treatment by the different narrative devices of the novel—the romantic primitive story is told in the first person by a sympathetic Easterner, while the success story is told in the third person.[8] G. Edward White argues that Wister desired "to integrate the Old West and the new order of the East in the person of his horseman of the plains . . . [He wanted] to combine the best features of nature and civilization, rugged individualism and gentlemanliness, past and present, and East and West into a more perfect whole. He suggests in the marriage of Molly and the Virginian that the 'true American' traditions of the eastern seaboard will constantly be revitalized as they pass westward, creating an even stronger and more unified nation."[9] The end of the novel confirms this theory for we see the Virginian turn capitalist "with a strong grip on many various enterprises." The country and the economy are revitalized by strong, rugged men bred in the West and polished by contact with Eastern culture. Surely this is the symbolic point to be made in noting that the novel is dedicated to Theodore Roosevelt, the Roughrider turned president.

So much for the implicit and explicit symbolism of the novel. What is now of interest is how the two film versions of this story changed or altered Wister's intended synthesis of East and West. The first film version of *The Virginian*, directed by Victor Fleming, was made in 1929 and starred Gary Cooper as the Virginian, Richard Arlen as Steve, Walter Huston as Trampas and Mary Brian as Molly. The film is a curious blend of the authentic and the amateur which makes many films of this period seem more realistic. The black and white print establishes the bleakness of the Western landscape. Many of the "takes" appear as if they were shot with a home movie camera. Everything is obviously "real": there are no studio shots. The exteriors, the interiors, the costumes, the cows, the dulled report of gunshots, the noise of the train drowning out dialogue, all establish the authenticity of the stark life which is portrayed on the screen.

The film opens with a picture of the Virginian at work, singing in a half-mumbled manner a tuneless cowboy song as he drives his cattle into town. There he meets Steve, his old crony, and they go into the saloon to have a drink. The Virginian is already a foreman, something it took Wister half a novel to accomplish; Steve, on the other hand, is still "the same." As the two men "dangle" around the bar, slapping each other on the back, drinking toasts to those wilder days when they "pulled that stuff" down by the border, we become aware of the psychological distance between the two men. Steve remains what the Virginian was before he became a foreman. The Virginian still has a great deal of the wild innocent in him, but becoming a foreman has established him as a member of the forces of seriousness. This membership has not yet been solidified, however, for the Virginian still finds a challenge in competing with Steve for the temporary affections of a barmaid. When Trampas enters the contest for the girl's affection and provokes the near confrontation which results in the famous line, "When you call me that, smile," the scene seems to establish the equality of the three men—each man wanted the same object and fought for it in the traditional Western manner. In a sense then, the film remains true to the novel. In the novel the famous line was uttered in a card game when the Virginian and Trampas were competing for the same pot. Barmaids and cards both entertain men of the West.

The intrusion of Eastern culture in the person of Molly Wood does not seem to alter the mood of gamesmanship apparent in the first scene. The Virginian and Steve have simply substituted Molly for the barmaid. When Steve is able to best the Virginian by uncovering the Virginian's trick, he is hardly able to smother a childish guffaw. Later, at a party given in Molly's honor, the trick and guffaws continue as both men are frustrated by the new school marm's culture. Steve dances clumsily and the Virginian cannot carry on a conversation with Molly without excessive stammering. Frustration leads to practical joking. The party for the new school teacher is also the occasion for a mass christening of newborn babies. As the ranch hand Honey says, christening is a sign that the country is "getting fancy." Reacting to the frustrations of the evening, the Virginian and Steve exchange the babies and therefore frustrate the christening.

The fact that there was no love triangle in Wister's novel is, I think, unimportant. But that information certainly helps us explain Steve's function in the film. He represents the Old West, the unenlightened West, the masculine, anarchistic, romantic and primitive West of the first half of Wister's novel. He is an image of what the Virginian was, and represents the kind of life for which the Virginian still has a degree of affection and nostalgia. But the Virginian, while still childish enough by Eastern standards to be equated with the boys in Molly's schoolroom, has demonstrated some interest in education. Immediately after the dance we see Molly in the schoolhouse attempting to lead a song. She is trying, in other words, to impose the harmony and order of civilization on the children of Medicine Bow. The Virginian sticks his head in the window and Molly, distracted by his presence, waves her hands in such a way as to destroy the harmony and order of the song she was trying to direct. It seems clear then that the Virginian's sexual vitality will eventually make his initial clumsiness insignificant and allow him to conquer. In the next scene the Virginian and Molly go riding in the mountains. When they stop, the Virginian sits on the ground while Molly sits on a rock. Her position above him is appropriate to the discussion of Shakespeare which follows. In the Virginian's eyes Romeo was a fairly decent hero except that he wasted a lot of time around the balcony. "If he wanted Juliet why didn't he take her?"

This picture of the Virginian counters Wister's portrait of him in the novel. The fictional hero accepted the rules of a leisurely and lengthy courtship, was duly impressed by Molly's education and cultural superiority. But Gary Cooper is not interested in play acting. He tells Molly to be real. He stands up, thus suggesting that he has attained if not superiority at least equality to Molly, kisses her, and proposes marriage. He tells her that teaching school is not a real woman's job. He suggests that they both go West and "do out there what the Judge did here . . . make United States out of prairie land." It is Molly who now feels clumsy. She says she feels like an outsider and realizes that she has more to learn before she can understand the West.

Ironically it is Steve, and therefore the image of what the Virginian used to be, who intrudes on this scene. The Virginian discovers Steve rustling, but their confrontation is easy and friendly. The Virginian admits that they have done a lot of "loco things" together, but "there are some things that are wrong." He suggests that the whole country is beginning to take things more seriously and that Steve should too. Steve's response is characteristic: "How do I know what I am going to do?" He then argues that the country is getting too civilized, that he will move West, and rides away singing "carry me back to the lone prairie." The importance of this scene is the Virginian's attitude toward Steve. He is not critical, ethical or patronizing. He simply preaches common sense and implies, in a friendly way, that Steve follow the example that he is beginning to set. That Steve chooses to leave rather than conform is not a significant or surprising event.

The point of all this is that Cooper plays the Virginian as an easygoing Western Romeo completely at home in his own environment. He does win Molly, but he does not need to change his cultural allegiance to the West in order to win her. In other words, we are not aware of that decisive movement toward the Eastern establishment and capitalistic respectability which Houghton identified as a major theme in the novel. Even when the Virginian is forced to punish Steve, forced to become serious, he does so within the context of the Western experience. Steve certainly understands the nature of that experience: when he is captured he utters a soliloquy on the meaning of life. It is, according to Steve, the simple cycle of nature, a few girls and a few drinks and death—"might as well be now as later." But what is dominant in the whole hanging episode is the contrast between Steve's affected jolliness and the Virginian's sudden seriousness. The quail's whistle, which has been their sign of friendship, is heard throughout the scene, thus reminding each of what had been before things got so serious. But the hanging is more a part of the Western ethic than it is a procedure of civilization. Hanging is a custom of the country and it is known and accepted by all. Steve has played the game and lost. To be sure, Cooper's face registers near nausea throughout the hanging, and Honey says that they would rather not hang Steve, but no one suggests leniency. The Virginian directs the hanging, faces Steve and the responsibility for the unfortunate event.

Further proof that the hanging is to be seen as part of the Western experience is documented by the moral revulsion it causes Molly. Soon after the hanging she discovers the children she has been trying to civilize acting out a mock hanging in the school yard, and thus hears about what the Virginian "had to do" to Steve. We also learn that both Steve and the Virginian were true to the code of the West because they did not act like "babies" when they confronted death. Mrs. Taylor is given the job of explaining the code to Molly. But she puts the West on a take-it-or-leave-it basis—this is the code; this is why it has to be; if you can't take it, get out. Molly begins by arguing that violence makes people hard—destroys their human feelings—but by the end of the scene she has become the equal of Mrs. Taylor. She argues that her family knows how to do things when they need to be done and offers their gallant deeds in the New York State Indian wars as proof. The scene closes as Molly expels Mrs. Taylor from the house. Molly has become worthy of her Western Romeo.

The final showdown with Trampas produces another crisis. The fight had been inevitable from the first scene of the film. And since that first confrontation was over something neither man really cared about—a barmaid—we know that neither man needs an issue to provoke a fight. If there is an issue, it is vengeance—the Virginian uses Steve's gun to kill Trampas, thus suggesting that the fight is an act of revenge. But really this version of the film makes clear that the duel is about honor. Molly says "it's just pride," but the Virginian says that unless he faces Trampas, he can never face Molly again. When the shooting is over, Molly runs into the street, kisses the Virginian and the film ends. There is no romantic finale, no sunsets, no music—just the kiss.

What this version of The Virginian accomplishes, then, it seems to me, is to present us with only the romantic cowboy hero; it gives us a brief glimpse of his move toward seriousness and education, but leaves us with essentially the same character at the end of the film. If anyone has changed it has been Molly—she has accepted the

West. The 1946 version of *The Virginian,* directed by Stuart Gilmore, gives us the other half of the Virginian's character. That is, if the Cooper film shows us the Virginian as cowboy Romeo, the 1946 version, which stars Joel McCrea as the Virginian, Sonny Tufts as Steve, Brian Donlevy as Trampas and Barbara Britton as Molly, gives us the Virginian as capitalist.

The most striking difference between the two films is one of tone. The 1946 version is in color and is packaged in the formula of the 1940s melodrama. The film is basically a studio picture: there are model trains instead of real trains, cowboys talking in front of a screen on which we see film clips of the cattle they are supposed to be herding, backdrops of the Tetons that resemble National Park Service postcards more than the real exteriors. There is also a great deal of emphasis on the ornate. The costumes are done by Edith Head. The homely attire of the 1929 film is replaced by high fashion gowns, suit coats and black string ties. The welcome party for Molly, for example, is no longer outside at the roughhewn picnic table, but inside in a beautifully decorated Victorian living room. The main feature of the 1946 version which establishes its tonal aura is its dependence on two classic soap opera techniques—closeup stares into the camera, and "significant" music. In each case what is being avoided is any meaningful attempt to resolve tensions, explain motivation or render the true context of the inward dilemma. On the other hand, the use of meaningful and wistful stares into the camera, the interpretive manipulation of events by music, may suggest that there are more tensions, motivations, and inward dilemmas than were existent in the 1929 version.

The opening of the 1946 version is symbolic of the change in emphasis which has been given to the story. We begin in Vermont where Molly is shown leaving her family in search of adventure. We see her prudish boyfriend, but his comment—"my family's counting on me marrying you"—suggests his limitations as a man. We then follow Molly's train West toward her rendezvous with romance and self-fulfillment. To state the matter differently, in the 1929 version, the eye of the camera, the "I" of the narrative, is certainly the Virginian, which may account for the resolution in favor of the West. But in the 1946 version it is Molly who becomes the implicit center of consciousness. We should therefore not be surprised when the movie ends not with a synthesis of East and West but a capitulation in favor of the East.

This capitulation is apparent in the first few scenes of the film. Steve and the Virginian meet *as* Molly's train pulls into town: Eastern culture does not intrude on pre-existing relationships as it did in the 1929 version, but is the occasion for bringing people together. After Steve and the Virginian fail in their initial attempt to win Molly, they retire to the bar. But Molly's presence invades even this oasis of masculine culture. Trampas tries to send a hospitable drink up to Molly's room. The Virginian takes this as an insult to the sacred institution of womanhood, defends Molly's honor and thus provokes the near fight and the famous line about "smiling" which was produced in the 1929 version by competition for a barmaid.

This alteration in plot is indicative of a change in the portrayal of the character of the Virginian. What we do not see in the 1946 version is that rakish, joking Virginian who could "dangle" around a bar contesting for barmaids. In fact, much of the joking around is eliminated from the 1946 version: the baby exchange is cut, for example. Also gone from the 1946 version is any indication that education is necessary for the Virginian. He is already the cultural equal of Molly. When they go for their ride in the mountains, there is no need to discuss books. They simply sit together by an Edenic pond—the Virginian sits slightly higher—and Molly listens to the Virginian spin his ambitious dream of success. Joel McCrea's Virginian is a serious man, stiff and puritanical in appearance. He is not shy or clumsy; he is a self-assured and confident businessman who will soon imitate the model of his boss, the Judge, and become a capitalist.

Nowhere is this change in the Virginian more evident than in his relationship with Steve. Steve is portrayed as the epitome of childish naiveté; the Virginian's paternalistic didacticism toward Steve shows the extent to which he has become the victim of ultimate seriousness. When the Virginian catches Steve rustling this change becomes manifest. Cooper and Arlen played this scene as equals, but McCrea and Tufts play the scene like Sunday school teacher and truant boy. Steve objects to the inquisitional tone of the affair by saying that the Virginian "takes life too seriously" and besides "you ain't my pappy." But these objections do not register with the Virginian, who has chosen to stand with the forces of law and order, the civilized establishment. His only interest is to impress upon Steve the desirability of making the same choice.

The significance of all this melodramatic preaching reaches a

climax when we come to the hanging scene. Suddenly the pace of
the movie retards considerably. Steve continues to express carefree
courage in the face of death, but the Virginian is significantly
changed. In the Cooper film we were aware of the impact of the
event because the Virginian suddenly got serious. In the McCrea
film we have already seen the Virginian serious. The change in the
Virginian's character is registered by his sudden desire to avoid the
event which he knew was inevitable. Rather than direct the
hanging himself, as Cooper did, McCrea moves on the outskirts of
the action in an attempt to shun participation. The zoom closeups
of characters staring meaningfully into the camera, which has been
a major melodramatic technique throughout the film, is given an
ironic twist in this scene. When the horses are whipped out from
under the hanging man, the camera zooms to a closeup of
McCrea's back. For all his preaching the Virginian has refused to
take ethical responsibility for his actions.

The character of Molly is also changed as played by Barbara
Britton. Perhaps a scene from the welcome party is illustrative: a
boy, attempting to prove that he can read, recites a label off a
baking powder container—"100 Percent Pure. Never Varies."
Molly comes West looking for adventure, but her character does
not vary. Her reaction to the news of Steve's hanging is
predictable—particularly since the music interprets for us the
meaning of her blank stare. When Mrs. Taylor explains the code,
Molly is reduced to tears and wants to leave. Unlike the earlier
Molly, who defended herself and then expelled Mrs. Taylor, this
Molly tries a weak defense, leaves town and then is brought back to
Medicine Bow by Andy, the stage driver. No resolution is offered;
Andy utters some inarticulate sentimentality that evokes the corny
reversal. What we see contradicts what we are supposed to see. We
are supposed to see that Molly has "spunk" and can learn to accept
the code of the West. What we see is a sentimental melodrama
where childish emotionalism rather than "spunk" occasions choice.

The ending of the film then is imminently predictable. It is
Trampas who has caused all the trouble. And we know from his
stereotyped black clothing that he must pay for the evil we see.
There was certainly an element of revenge in the Cooper-Huston
duel, but since we saw their initial confrontation over a barmaid
we know that finally the duel would be between two men who
needed no issue other than their honor over which to fight. Molly
objected to this fight because it had no obvious social purpose. But

when she saw the Virginian in danger she realized, as John G. Cawelti has suggested, "that her love was greater than her genteel antipathy to violence."[10] Since the film ends with Molly awarding the Virginian a kiss as he stands in the street with his gun smoking, we must conclude that the film ends with a confirmation of the code of the West.

The McCrea-Donlevy duel involves other motives. Revenge is certainly a more apparent motive and with good cause. The Virginian blames Trampas for leading Steve astray, but he also blames Trampas for Steve's death. More to the point, he blames Trampas for his own need to enforce the penalty of death on Steve. But since the Virginian has failed to face that death, his guilt is double—he has failed the code of the East by not enforcing the system of law and order he has preached about, and he has failed the code of the West by not facing death. This multiple guilt is transferred to Trampas. The Virginian has no desire to return to the freedom and violence of the West. He wishes to maintain the order and stability of the East. Trampas then becomes a threat and an unfortunate hurdle that must be overcome if order and stability are to remain. But overcoming this hurdle is only a minor act in a larger drama. As John G. Cawelti again points out,

> This resolution resembled the redefinition of the success ethic worked out under the impact of the new industrial society of the late nineteenth century. In this ethic the aggressiveness of the industrial entrepreneur and violent social dislocations of industrial growth were seen as a temporary phase; Andrew Carnegie summed up this ethical conception in his own career and in such writings as his famous "The Gospel of Wealth." According to Carnegie the individual should compete aggressively and ruthlessly for power and wealth which could then be used philanthropically for the benefit of society.[11]

All this seems to me implicit in the Virginian's execution of Trampas. The manipulation of weather and lighting during the duel—the high winds, the darkness—suggest an event of major importance. But it is only a temporary crisis. Once the violence is over, the Virginian and Molly ride off into the sunset with their goods on an extra packhorse. They are going West to settle and build an empire. But it is the East which has triumphed.

What is also being suggested here is that the Trampas-Virginian polarity is not as clear as it first seems. In the novel, Trampas was simply a ranchhand who had been passed over for promotion. Only after he spent all day drinking "courage" did he challenge the Virginian. In both films he is promoted to a rustler-rancher—a man who has his own brand. In the 1929 version, however, there is a suggestion of equality among the three male characters. Trampas does things which everybody did at one time. But he must cease to do these things since civilization is approaching. In the 1946 version Trampas is villain, devil, nemesis. Yet if this Trampas is antithetical to the Virginian, what is he? The Virginian, as we have seen, is an Eastern capitalist. Does this make Trampas the true Westerner? There is certainly a sense in which Trampas and Steve, if taken together, give us a complete picture of the West. If Steve represents the free individual, the primitive-romantic, Trampas represents the extension of those concepts to anarchism and outlawry. If Steve's wildness is a sign of his vitality, it is also a sign of the potentiality for sudden death which exists outside the secure and stable structure of society. And if Steve is innocence, Trampas is certainly knowledge. Trampas knows that the security and stability of society is only veneer and that no amount of Eastern culture will ever wipe away the realities of wildness and death. He knows that people come West for "health, wealth and bad reputation." In some ways the serious Virginian is as ignorant as the childish Steve because he refuses to try to integrate this knowledge into a new synthesis of East and West. Indeed, he refuses to face that knowledge. Instead of allowing the West to revitalize the East, he executes it.

The two films have therefore shown us that Wister's intended synthesis is too precarious to be kept in balance. The 1929 Virginian had not reached the point where the East was a significant force in his life. The 1946 Virginian must destroy the West in order that the East may survive. It seems that the further we get from the reality of the Western experience the greater become the changes in the content of the Western myth. The novel, written in 1902, gave classic formulation to the Western myth just as the reality of the Western frontier was ending. In his preface to the novel, Wister acknowledges the passing of the horseman of the plains and his way of life: "Such a transition was inevitable. Let us give thanks that it is but a transition and not a finality."[12]

Wister had hoped that the characteristic virtues of individuality typified by the Virginian would be able to survive in the new century. By the time of the 1929 film, such hopes could no longer be realistically entertained. World War I had initiated Americans into a new age, a complex age where the romantic gestures of individualism produced *nada*. Perhaps it is because of this initiation that Americans were ripe, as Roderick Nash has pointed out, for particular kinds of heroes.[13] Despite the acceleration of life in urban America in the '20s, the most popular writers of the decade, Zane Grey and Gene Stratton-Porter, focused on "frontier and rural patterns of thought."[14] The 1929 Virginian affirmed the traditional frontier virtues in the wake of the growing obsolescence of those virtues.

The 1940s were also a period of disillusionment. World War II, the concentration camps, Hiroshima, demonstrated the further decline in the possibilities for individuality. Americans had been forced out of their isolation and into a full international engagement in order to stop a menace, but overcoming the threat of that crisis did not resolve their problems. As Chester Eisinger has indicated, Americans returned to the

> . . . United States to discover that the corporate character of life here often mirrored the regimentation of the military and demanded much the same conformity. The society seemed to be dominated more and more by great corporate entities—business, government, labor and the peacetime military establishment—that provided a prefabricated place for the conforming individual if he would disguise himself or cut himself to fit such a place, thereby surrendering his individualism.[15]

In 1946, the Virginian is unfortunately at home in this kind of world. He is a disillusioned man who has decided to settle for security.

The Virginian's successive versions have thus documented the alteration in the character of the Western myth and our attitude toward it. In a way that has apparently escaped our conscious awareness, we have changed the myth. The love of romantic innocence, natural primitivism and rugged individualism has not been polished and perfected by contact with the East. Rather, the virtues of the West have been exchanged for the love of Victorian seriousness, cultural rigidity and the emergence of the corporate executive.

NOTES

1. "This march to the West is our Odyssey." Quoted in George N. Fenin and William K. Everson, *The Western: From Silents to Cinerama* (New York: Bonanza, 1962), p. 319.

2. Of course there are other versions of *The Virginian*. NBC had good success with two television series using the names of the characters, though little else, from the original story. Fenin and Everson speak of a road company version of the story *circa* 1900 which starred William S. Hart (*The Western*, p. 76). But for purposes of focus, I will restrict myself to the novel and the 1929 and 1946 film versions.

3. Robert Warshow, "The Westerner," in *The Immediate Experience* (New York: Doubleday, 1962), p. 137.

4. Warshow, p. 140.

5. Warshow, p. 141.

6. Donald Davis, "Ten Gallon Hero," *American Quarterly* 6 (Summer 1954):12.

7. Donald E. Houghton, "Two Heroes in One: Reflections on the Popularity of *The Virginian,"Journal of Popular Culture* 3 (Fall 1970):498–499.

8. Houghton, p. 498.

9. G. Edward White, *The Eastern Establishment and the Western Experience* (New Haven: Yale University Press, 1968), pp. 141–143.

10. John G. Cawelti, "The Gunfighter and Society," *The American West* 5 (March 1968):32.

11. Cawelti, p. 76.

12. Owen Wister, *The Virginian: A Horseman of the Plains* (New York: Macmillan, 1902), p. xi.

13. Roderick Nash, *The Nervous Generation: American Thought, 1917–1930* (Chicago: Rand McNally, 1970), p. 126.

14. Nash, p. 137.

15. Chester E. Eisinger, *The 1940's: Profile of a Nation in Crisis* (Garden City, New York: Doubleday, 1969), p. xvi.

3

STAGECOACH (1939)

David Clandfield

David Clandfield teaches at the University of Toronto, Toronto, Canada.

In the course of John Ford's *Stagecoach*,[1] the audience's attention is frequently drawn to names: the terror inspired by the name Geronimo, mentioned in the opening title (p. 25) and enacted in the opening sequence; the elusiveness of the whiskey drummer's name, Peacock (pp. 44, 64, 121, 133), for all Doc Boone's enthusiasm as he remarks, "a familiar name, an honoured name!" (p. 44); the explanation of a *nickname*, Ringo's (p. 56); the revelation of a *pseudonym*, Hatfield's (pp. 72, 129); the jocular choosing of a *name* for the baby born at Apache Wells, "Little Coyote" (pp. 98–99);[2] the prominently displayed *nameplate* of Doc Boone which he wrenches off the wall in Tonto (pp. 32, 41); the unsuspecting crooked banker proudly *naming* himself "Ellsworth H. Gatewood" in Lordsburg and triggering his own arrest (p. 135).

The frequent attention given to names seems even more striking when we compare Dudley Nichols's script with the short story by Ernest Haycox on which it is based.[3] In addition to structural changes, Nichols has changed many of the place-names and characters' names. Not all have been changed, nor have they been changed at random. While the terminal points of the journey (Tonto and Lordsburg) are retained, the intermediate stations have been altered; although the passengers' names have been changed

David Clandfield, "The Onomastic Code of *Stagecoach*," *Literature/Film Quarterly* 5 (Spring 1977). © 1977 by *Literature/Film Quarterly*. Reprinted by permission of the publisher.

completely, those of the adversaries remain the same (Geronimo and Plummer). The name changes may be schematized as follows:

	Haycox prototype	*Nichols version*
Places	Tonto	Tonto
	"midday relay station"	Dry Fork
	Gap Creek	Apache Wells
	Schriebers	East Ferry[4]
	Lordsburg	Lordsburg
People		
Passengers	Malpais Bill	The Ringo Kid/Henry
	Henriette	Dallas
	Miss Robinson	Mrs. Lucy Mallory
	(fiancée of Lt. Hauser)	(wife of Capt. Mallory)
	Johnny Strang	Curly [Wilcox][5]
	Happy Stuart	Buck [Rickabough]
	"the gambler"	Hatfield/Ringfield
	"the whiskey drummer"	[Samuel] Peacock
	---------	Josiah Boone, M.D.
	---------	Ellsworth H. Gatewood
Adversaries	Geronimo	Geronimo
	Plummer and Shanley	Plummer brothers

Given the overt emphasis accorded to names in the script and the systematic renaming of people and places, we are entitled to inquire whether the names themselves serve to illuminate the deeper structures of the plot. Does an analysis of Nichols's naming system reveal a structural pattern that lies within the ideological infrastructure of the script? I believe that it does. It should be understood, however, that the succeeding analysis is not to be evaluated in terms of the scriptwriter's overt intentions. It is based strictly on what we find in the script and see or hear in the film.

I shall begin by looking at the passenger list of the stagecoach and return to the place-names later. If we seek phonetic and semantic links that would separate passengers into smaller units, we quickly find a series of pairs.

The counterpart for Ringo is Hatfield, whose real name we learn is Ringfield. The common syllable RING is more than a phonetic link; its meaning is entirely appropriate as the emblematic reminder of the sentimental attraction each feels for one of the lady passengers (Ringo for Dallas, Hatfield for Lucy). The similarity does not stop here. Each, in his own way, is an outlaw; each came from a good family (pp. 69, 129); each has known bad times; each is proved courageous in the face of adversity (the Indian attack). Neither is commonly known by his real name, although, interestingly enough, it is Hatfield's *concealed name* which resembles Ringo's *nickname*. Whereas Ringo's true identity is indistinguishable in the film from his heroic *persona*, Hatfield's heroic stature only emerges in time of need. Having acquitted himself honorably, he is finally worthy, like the heroes of medieval romance, to name his true name; he is finally worthy to state the resemblance he bears to Ringo.

The names of the lady passengers who are the objects of attention, Dallas and Mrs. Mallory, are also phonetically linked but semantically opposed. The link is provided by the rhyming of the stressed syllable ALL; the traditional opposition of whore and mother is reinforced by the connotations of near homonyms (Dallas — dallies, dalliance — amorousness; Mallory — mammary — motherhood). Just as the semantic opposition is transformed and masked by the phonetic similarity, so the socially opposed roles of fallen woman and respectable cavalry officer's wife merge and are reconciled in the face of childbirth, the visible moment at which the consequences of amorousness are converted into the responsibilities of motherhood. This convergence is completed at the end of the film by Dallas's acceptance of married life with Ringo, as Lucy Mallory is reunited with her wounded husband. Dallas is phonetically coupled with Lucy's acquired name, her married name, the badge of her respectability. It is this badge that Dallas sets out to acquire with Ringo at the end.

The third pair is Buck, the driver, and Peacock, the whiskey drummer. The names nearly rhyme, and the common characteristic is thrown into relief by the variations on Peacock's name (Handcock, p. 64; Haycock, p. 44; and in Nichols's original script also Hitchcock, p. 146, and Petcock, p. 147) in which the syllable COCK is a constant. Not only are the names phonetically linked, but they are also semantically linked. Both are zoological, and both have sexually potent connotations ("buck," the male goat; "peacock," with its suggestions of exhibitionism and the male sex organ). These connotations are ironic for much of the film. Throughout most of the journey, each seems to be at the mercy or under the thumb of a more determined or a more aggressive character. Buck's protestations about the dangers of continuing the journey are always overruled by Curly (pp. 48, 50, 62), as are

Peacock's by Doc Boone (p. 49). Boone's aggressive consumption of Peacock's whiskey samples is paralleled by Buck's sorry observation that his Mexican wife has got him feeding half the state of Chihuahua (p. 51). Both then are butts or victims. The sexual connotation of their names is not entirely inappropriate: both have large families, a fact which, when revealed by Peacock, provokes the ironic rejoinder from Doc Boone: "Then you're a man! By all the powers that be, Reverend, you're a man" (p. 49). Both men emerge from their ordeal as wounded "heroes" bearing the visible signs of the skirmish; but more than that, each has enhanced his reputation with his fellow-travellers. When Boone next calls Peacock "a man" (p. 101), there is no trace of irony in his voice; Buck will play his part in the showdown with the Plummers despite his injury (p. 139). The film closes with the promise of family reunion for both men.

Where Gatewood and Doc Boone are concerned, the phonetic similarity is trivial; in fact, the –OO– is an orthographic similarity alone. Nevertheless, the two clearly form a pair. They are professional men each enouncing professional values:

> Gatewood: ". . . it's good sound business . . ." (p. 32) "What's good business for the banks is good for the country" (p. 32) ". . . as if we didn't know how to run our banks" (p. 70).
>
> Boone: "Professional compliments are always pleasing" (p. 57) ". . . don't look so proud, I've brought hundreds of 'em into the world" (p. 100) "If you want my professional opinion . . ." (p. 101).

Indeed, each of them has a tendency to moralize, and Boone calls himself at one point a "philosopher" (p. 63). In addition, both men's careers are seriously jeopardized in the film (Boone kicked out of Tonto, Gatewood arrested in Lordsburg). Each in turn annoys Hatfield for his lack of consideration for Lucy Mallory (Boone for smoking, pp. 57–58; Gatewood for wanting to continue the journey regardless of Lucy's health, pp. 97–98, 101–102). As they are leaving, we realize ironically that each is fleeing the same harridan, Mrs. Gatewood, whose associations with the Law and Order League bring no joy to either Boone (pp. 42, 52) or Gatewood (p. 45). Both are leaving behind unpaid debts (Boone's unpaid rent; Gatewood's stolen payroll).

Nevertheless, Boone and Gatewood are clearly distinguished and opposed and not only by the reactions each provokes in the spectator. Gatewood is characterized by a *surface* of professionalism; Boone by a *surface* of drunken incompetence:

Gatewood: "What the country needs is a businessman for President."
Boone: "What the country needs is more bottle" (p. 70).

In the hour of danger, Gatewood's surface is cracked to reveal his incapabilities, while Boone's is cracked to reveal his professional ability:

Boone: "Gatewood, will you shut up! I've got a patient here!"
Gatewood: "Stop this stage! Let me out of here" (p. 123).

However, it is in their names that the contrast is most clearly revealed. Josiah Boone (his name is revealed in full on his nameplate, p. 32, and in conversation, p. 63) has the ideal name for an obstetrician: *Josiah* means "may God heal" (referring to the woman in childbirth),[6] *Boone* recalls *boon*, "blessings." Ellsworth H. Gatewood (as he calls himself on p. 135) needs but the slightest transposition of letters to produce *Hellsworth* and *Hategood*. By this opposition of names Boone, healer and lifegiver, takes on a divine identity, whereas Gatewood, the dishonest moneydealer, takes on a Satanic identity.

There remains but one traveller on the stage: Curly, the marshal riding shotgun. One, that is, unless we include the child that is born at Apache Wells, but the latter is hardly a character but rather a precious cargo. If we consider Curly's role in the denouement of the film, we do find his counterpart.

The marshal is, in fact, the agent who permits Ringo's revenge-quest to proceed to its successful conclusion. But the film contains two denouements, for earlier the dramatic rescue of the stagecoach from the Apaches had taken place. Here the *deus ex machina* is the cavalry. The cavalry is, of course, the institutional military counterpart of the marshal, Curly. Curly and cavalry are almost anagrams, phonetically and orthographically. Although the cavalry only accompanies the stage at the beginning and end of the journey, it is of course on everyone's mind throughout.

The pairings are then complete. We can construct from them the following grid:

Name	Social Role	*Dramatic* Function	*Name-* Value
RINGo-RINGfield	outlaw (redeemed)	lady's protector	P = S =
dALLas-mALLory	woman (mother)	lady needing protection	P = S ≠
bUCK-peacOCK	family man and traveller	butt/victim	P = S =
bOOne-gatewOOd	professional man (ruined?)	moralist	(P=) S ≠
cuRLY-CavaLRY	law keeper	*deus ex machina*	P = S =

(P phonetic; S semantic; = similarity; ≠ opposition)

So far we have been discussing the paired characteristics along the horizontal axes of this grid. If we now view the two columns of names vertically, it is not difficult to discern a series of antinomies that hold the left side apart from the right side when each is taken as a group.

The characters found on the left side each embody one or several of the following qualities or aspirations: individualism, simplicity, crudity, independence, integrity, sincerity, resourcefulness, egalitarianism, self-awareness. The characters on the right side each embody one or several of the following qualities or aspirations: refinement, institutionalization, self-delusion, corruption, legalism, class-consciousness, capitalism. These characteristics are also distributed through the structural grid of values postulated for the Western as a genre by Jim Kitses in *Horizons West.*[7] I reproduce it here for reference:

WILDERNESS	CIVILIZATION
Individual	*Community*
freedom	restriction
honor	institutions
self-knowledge	illusions
integrity	compromise
self-interest	social responsibility
solipsism	democracy
Nature	*Culture*
purity	corruption
experience	knowledge

empiricism	legalism
pragmatism	idealism
brutalization	refinement
savagery	humanity
The West	*The East*
America	Europe
the frontier	America
equality	class
agrarianism	industrialism
tradition	change
the past	the future

No one character has to embody characteristics from all these subdivisions, since each of the three divisions proposed offers a wide range of values going from the negative to the positive or vice versa. Nor can the grid be used to account for plot *development*, since it offers the basis for a dialectical structure without imposing a necessary resolution or synthesis. In my analysis to this point, I have chosen to examine a structure operating at the level of character relationships (with the characters coded according to their names, their social roles, and their dramatic functions). When we apply the criteria of the Kitses grid, we find that two groups emerge united vertically and opposed horizontally.

Nevertheless, as we have seen, although the groups are ideologically opposed, the horizontal pairs often share traits, form alliances, or at the least experience no mutual hostility. This does not weaken the validity of the Kitsean grid. The harmony created in the Concord stagecoach in the face of danger (except for the Satanic banker) is a symptom of the gradual shift of the conflict between Wilderness and Civilization on to a more abstract and broader scale (savage versus white man).

It is in analyzing the shift of the conflict from the social to the abstract and back to the social again that we become aware of the value of the new place-names that Nichols has added.

Back at Tonto, the starting point, the two groups of travellers were clearly distinguished. There were those who travelled voluntarily (Lucy, Peacock, Gatewood, Hatfield) and those whose departure was involuntary (Dallas, Boone, and later Ringo) or necessary (Buck as driver, Curly as shotgun).

The stage left from the Oriental Saloon, a reminder of the "Eastern"[8] status of a town where the Law and Order League holds sway and where the bank does a thriving business. It is due to arrive at the El Dorado in Lordsburg, a more traditional "Western" town with its poker games, red-light district, and sensational newspaper. Lordsburg is a town of the night, Tonto is seen in blazing sunlight. Those who make it to El Dorado will have had to survive the perilous journey across the wilderness and deserve the rewards that their safe arrival may bring.

The Perilous Journey takes the coach through a series of stations whose names underline the hostility of the environment: Dry Fork and the desert, Apache Wells and Indian territory, the crossing of East Ferry into the most hostile "Western" tract that the coach must negotiate. As these threatening outside forces progressively assert themselves, the internal divisions within the coach almost merge into concord.

At Lordsburg, with the danger past, there is a new parting of the ways for the passengers. The true "Westerners" are united in the showdown with the Plummers, from which the "Easterners" are excluded: Curly allows Ringo to pursue his revenge while Dallas agonizes over his fate; Buck conveys Ringo's challenge to the Plummers; Doc Boone relieves Luke of his shotgun in the bar. The "Easterners" for their part are much the worse for wear: Hatfield is dead; Peacock and Lucy are stretcher cases; Gatewood is arrested.

The farewells between "Easterners" and "Westerners" (Mallory/Dallas, p. 131; Peacock/Dallas, p. 133) are little more than formulae, however sincerely offered. The farewell within the "Westerners" group, as Dallas and Ringo ride off "saved . . . from the blessings of civilization" (p. 143), is a strong affirmation of the "Western" ideology.

The operative structure of Nichols's *Stagecoach* is then indeed the Wilderness/Civilization conflict or opposition that many critics have observed. What distinguishes this film from many other "classic" Westerns is the duality of levels at which this dialectic operates.

The broader level pits the white man against the savage, both reduced in the excitingly shot action sequences to almost homogeneous abstractions. This level is also maintained in the second denouement, where the conflict is between the positive "Westerners" (acting in concert in Lordsburg) and the negative "Westerners" (the Plummers). For this abstract level of the plot, which provides a starting point and a double conclusion for the film, Nichols has retained the framework and, for the adversaries, the names of the Haycox short story.

Within the stagecoach, a new level of conflict has been developed. The tensions are strongest at the outset, but as the more abstract level of conflict asserts itself, they are eclipsed temporarily until the conclusion when the division is re-established. This social level of conflict is largely the invention of Nichols and has engendered a new onomastic system to go with it. This renaming does more than serve as a point of departure for something new. It embodies much of the richness and complexity of the characters' relationships as they are developed both dramatically and ideologically.[9]

NOTES

1. John Ford and Dudley Nichols, *Stagecoach* (New York: Simon and Schuster, 1971). Page references are taken from this edition of the script. In discussing the film, I refer to Nichols as the author in order to emphasize my focus on the diagetic elements of plot and dialogue to the virtual exclusion of cinematographic elements such as shot composition, editing, music, etc.

2. This naming sequence was omitted from the final version of the film. It is included in the notes of the published filmscript, pp. 148–149.

3. Ernest Haycox, "Stage to Lordsburg," *Collier's*, April 10, 1937, pp. 18–19; reprinted in the published filmscript, pp. 5–18.

4. It is referred to first as Lee Ferry (p. 45), but subsequently as East Ferry (pp. 67, 109).

5. The square brackets enclose those names which appear in the script but are not heard in the film. They are not discussed further.

6. See E. G. Wythycombe, *Oxford Dictionary of English Christian Names* (London: Oxford University Press, 1963), p. 173.

7. Jim Kitses, *Horizons West* (Bloomington: Indiana University Press, 1969), p. 11.

8. The terms "Eastern(er)" and "Western(er)" are used figuratively as in Kitses's grid, without precise or literal geographical meaning. Indeed, the coach journey proceeds Eastward geographically but Westward dramatically and ideologically. Similarly, Boone, the Yankee, and Hatfield, the Southern gentleman, may be incorporated into the grid as "Westerner" and "Easterner" on ideological grounds.

9. Both Nichols's script and the Haycox story derive ultimately from Maupassant's *Boule de Suif*, as has been remarked on numerous occasions. In that story, too, a similar onomastic coding may be observed, but it is much weaker and semantic only.

4

FORT APACHE (1948)

William T. Pilkington

William T. Pilkington is professor of English at Tarleton State University, Stephenville, Texas. He is the author of My Blood's Country: Studies in Southwestern Literature *(1973) and* Harvey Fergusson *(1975).*

Fort Apache,[1] though it has been highly praised by several auteur critics enamored of the work of John Ford, falls considerably short of being Ford's finest Western. Viewed within the context of the director's Westerns, the film projects neither the classic simplicity of *Stagecoach* (1939) nor the rich complexity of *The Searchers* (1956). It may be argued that the 1948 movie is not even the best of Ford's so-called "cavalry trilogy"—the other titles being *She Wore a Yellow Ribbon* (1949) and *Rio Grande* (1950). Nevertheless *Fort Apache* is an interesting and important motion picture, a pivotal point, I think, in the development of Ford's understanding and portrayal of the Western experience, particularly the place of the Indian in that experience.

The plot of *Fort Apache* is mostly standard Western fare, full of Indian battles and breathtaking cavalry charges. Owen Thursday (Henry Fonda) is a Civil War general who has been demoted to the rank of lieutenant colonel and banished to the provinces, where he is assigned command of Fort Apache, an outpost in the desert. He brings with him to the new command his lovely daughter Philadelphia (Shirley Temple). Thursday is resentful at having been sent to such an isolated, uncivilized place; and partly to soothe his

© 1979 by the University of New Mexico Press.

ruffled feelings, partly no doubt for reasons best explained by
Freud, he overzealously attempts to suppress the budding romance
between Philadelphia and Lieutenant Michael O'Rourke (John
Agar), who is deemed to be socially inferior to the Thursdays and
therefore unacceptable.

At his new post Thursday very quickly sees a chance to redeem
himself—to regain his former rank and reputation—when he learns,
pretty much by accident, that Cochise is a name familiar to readers
of Eastern newspapers. Cochise (Miguel Inclan) is, it seems, safely
ensconced with a large band of his followers across the border in
Mexico, not far from Fort Apache. The commander sends Captain
Kirby York (John Wayne), whom Cochise trusts, to set up a friendly
meeting with the Indians. Thursday double-crosses both York and
Cochise by bringing along to the conclave the full complement of
cavalry troops under his command and by summarily ordering the
Apache chieftain and his braves to return to the reservation. When
Cochise refuses, Thursday and the cavalry attack. The Indians,
however, have prepared a trap which is so successful that the
entire cavalry unit, including Thursday, is annihilated. York,
Lieutenant O'Rourke, and a few others, because they have acted
honorably, are spared.

The film's coda, which takes place several years after the
climactic battle, shows York, who now commands the fort, talking
to a group of newspaper reporters. Behind him hangs an elegant
portrait of Colonel Thursday. A reporter comments that Thursday
"must have been a great man"; York replies, rather curtly, that "no
man died more gallantly." When the reporters concoct a highly
romanticized description of Thursday's last battle, the officer
affirms that this account is "correct in every detail." York asserts, in
sum, that "We are a better troop because of him." Rather
inexplicably, then, York covers up Thursday's blunder, making his
late commander appear the epitome of bravery and heroism.

When it was released in 1948, most reviewers saw *Fort Apache* as
a simple—not to say simple-minded—Western, to be enjoyed for the
visual delights of its action sequences, but hardly for its intellectual
stimulation. The *New York Times* dismissed the movie as a "rootin',
tootin' Wild West show."[2] The review of the film (unsigned but
probably written by James Agee) that appeared in *Time* magazine
called it "an unabashed potboiler." *Time* also charged that the
picture was guilty of "some of the bleakest Irish comedy and
sentimentality since the death of vaudeville."[3] This last comment

refers mainly to the dialogue exchanged by Lieutenant O'Rourke's father, Sergeant Major O'Rourke (Ward Bond), and Sergeant Mulcahy (Victor McLaglen); certainly the Irish accents and the blarney in these scenes are exaggerated enough that *Time*'s criticism isolates a real, if minor, flaw in the movie.

Without question *Fort Apache* has its weak spots. The cavils and generally trivial complaints of reviewers, however, do not adequately define or explain those weaknesses. The primary failure in the film, it seems to me, derives from Ford's ambivalent view of his subject. Now ambivalence in a work of art, if rightly handled, can add immeasurably to the aesthetic effectiveness of that work. In *Fort Apache* it merely issues into confusion. The movie is not, as has been claimed, "a belated recruiting picture for the Army,"[4] but Ford undoubtedly made the film with the intention of celebrating the role of the cavalry in the winning of the West. He felt that in the past too many Westerns (his own *Stagecoach* is a case in point) had shown the cavalry only as an undifferentiated collective *deus ex machina*, galloping to the rescue at the crucial moment, dispatching the pesky redskins, and then discreetly receding into the background. Ford wanted to uncover the human truth that lay hidden beneath the familiar stereotype—to show how life, both institutional and personal, was really lived on a frontier outpost.

When he began searching for "truth," Ford's honesty would not allow him to ignore the disparity that usually separates legend from reality—the fact that the actions of many a "hero" have hardly been predicated on the principles of heroism, not to mention common sense. It is almost as if, having explored this idea through most of the movie, the director suddenly remembered his original purpose: to celebrate the indispensable part played by the cavalry in the advance of civilization across the American West and to affirm the institution's importance, no matter the weaknesses of its individual components. To fulfill that purpose, he had only one alternative—a tricky double reverse which results in the film's curious ending. The odd thing is, as Russell Campbell points out, that Ford asserts a "faith in myth" at the close of a "movie whose concern has been exposing myth to get at the truth."[5]

At the center of Ford's difficulties in *Fort Apache* is the character of Owen Thursday, memorably portrayed by Henry Fonda. Though the name and setting have been changed, Thursday's story is, of course, Ford's version of the legend of Col. George Armstrong Custer. Like Custer, Thursday is ambitious for fame and glory. Like

Custer, he is foolhardy, lacking knowledge of or respect for the unconventional but often effective tactics of his enemies. And like Custer's, his excessive ambition and ignorance lead to disaster. Ford's camera shows Thursday to be a completely believable human being, but it also mercilessly reveals him as not a very likable one. He is often arrogant in the handling of his men, disregarding advice from those (usually Captain York) who know more than he does. He is unfeeling in denying the emotional needs of his daughter (who nonetheless continues to love him) in favor of the forms of Victorian respectability. In short, the viewer finds it difficult to dispute James Agee's alliterative description of Thursday as a "megalomaniacal martinet."[6]

Ironies, great and small, continually undercut Thursday's sense of his own importance. At the beginning of the film he pompously lectures Captain Collingwood (George O'Brien) that the Captain ought to be familiar with Robert E. Lee's paper on "the trap" as a military tactic. "The trap"—as executed by the Apaches—turns out to be the instrument of Thursday's doom. At another point, having insultingly rejected Lieutenant O'Rourke's family background as insufficient to match his daughter's genteel breeding, Thursday ironically finds himself obliged to dance with the Lieutenant's mother, Mrs. O'Rourke (Irene Rich), at the non-commissioned officers' ball, a task he performs with ill-concealed distaste; to carry the irony further, form also calls for the father, Sergeant Major O'Rourke, to dance with Philadelphia. The audience relishes Thursday's discomfort, having seen in virtually every situation in the film his disagreeable personality.

How, then, to account for the movie's conclusion? It is, in my view, a conclusion almost as schizophrenic as that of a popular 1950s film, *The Caine Mutiny*, in which the infamous Captain Queeg is ridiculed throughout, viewed as an object of contempt, and finally shown to be quite insane. In the end, though, those responsible for the Captain's fall are morally indicted and Queeg defended for his long and unstinting service to the U.S. Navy. The reversal at the close of *The Caine Mutiny*, however—as in *Fort Apache*—does not work because it is unsupported by preceding events; the concluding "message" is simply inconsistent with what we have *seen* in the course of the movie. In a recent interview John Wayne, who played Captain York in *Fort Apache*, suggests that he was not unaware of the problems created by the film's conclusion. Concerning York's cover-up of Thursday's blunder, Wayne comments, "I think the character was saying that because the newspapermen were asking him things . . . . [York] finally is forced to say something, and I thought it was good because it doesn't say he was a great guy and it certainly doesn't say that he was a bastard. It's about the least provocative thing he could say about that man, one way or the other."[7] A small but significant detail, however, makes Wayne's explanation seem at best incomplete: following his exchange with the reporters York wears Thursday's distinctive hat as he leads the troops out on a new mission (to round up Geronimo and his warriors). Perhaps, as Wayne says, York in the news conference was only supplying inane answers to reporters' inane questions, but he shortly thereafter appears consciously to place himself in a line of succession that follows Thursday's example. And that, I insist, is scarcely consistent with York's character, as it has been established throughout most of the film.

At any rate, it is perfectly all right for York, in rationalizing his bending of the truth to enhance Thursday's posthumous reputation, to imply that what is crucial is the institution of the cavalry and not the success or failure of any individual officer; we may agree or disagree with that premise, but it is at least a defensible position. It is also acceptable for Ford himself to believe, as he has said in connection with *Fort Apache*, that "it's good for the country to have heroes to look up to"[8]—even if they are not really heroes at all. The problem arises, I contend, in somehow embedding these ideas in a film. They ought to be implicit in every scene and character in the movie, not afterthoughts incongruously tacked on at the conclusion. The overt message of *Fort Apache* is, unfortunately, little more than just such a disconcerting and puzzling afterthought, which results in an inevitable diminution of the aesthetic pleasure the viewer has to that point derived from the film.

But if the movie has clearly visible defects, it also possesses its considerable virtues. Those virtues are characteristically Fordian. One of them certainly is the director's careful attention to detail—his unswerving fidelity to time and place. To begin with, the camera, under Ford's expert direction, faithfully records the stark beauty—the immemorial buttes and mesas—of Monument Valley, Arizona, Ford's favorite location for shooting Westerns. One can easily understand why he liked the place so much; it is an awe-inspiring landscape, a veritable geographic microcosm of the

West. Frank S. Nugent, who wrote the script for *Fort Apache*, tells a whimsical story that, in its punch line, belies the care Ford actually took to prepare for making the film. According to Nugent, the director

> gave me a list of about fifty books to read—memoirs, novels, anything about the period. Later he sent me down into the old Apache country to nose around, get the smell and feel of the land. I got an anthropology graduate at the University of Arizona as a guide, and we drove around—out to the ruins of Fort Bowie, and through Apache Pass where there are still the markers "Killed by Apaches" and the dates. When I got back, Ford asked me if I had done enough research. I said yes. "Good," he said. "Now just forget everything you've read, and we'll start writing a movie."[9]

Even seemingly insignificant particulars had to be "right"; not many Westerns, I would guess, require, as did *Fort Apache*, full-time choreographers and "costume researchers" among the filming teams.

Another strength of the movie is the authentic sense of everyday life that it projects. The people, professional relationships, and domestic arrangements that exist within the confines of the fort are pictured in detail. We feel that this is the way life was—or could well have been—inside an isolated outpost during the latter half of the nineteenth century. Numerous critics have remarked on Ford's concern, in his Westerns, for showing the importance of the community and its function as a fragile oasis of human values in the vast emptiness of the wilderness. Russell Campbell is right on target, I think, in employing a sociological concept to explain what Ford had in mind in creating the intricate society of Fort Apache. It is a society that closely resembles the "organic community" formulated by Ferdinand Tönnies in his classic *Gemeinschaft und Gesellschaft*. Campbell's gloss summarizes Tönnies's basic idea:

> Gemeinschaft ("community") is described as a type of social organization prevalent in a pre-industrial society, character-ized by unity, strong bonds of kinship and friendship, relative peace, close ties to the land, home production and barter, and a flourishing of folk arts. In contrast is Gesellschaft ("assoca-tion"), the modern world of atomization, breakdown of the family and personal alienation, wars of mass slaughter, high geographical mobility, commercialism, and science.[10]

Ford obviously favors—or at least carefully recreates—the first type of society. (Tönnies's construction of opposing kinds of social arrangements is, of course, a more generalized way of looking at the Western community versus the Eastern city.)

The director spends a good deal of time in *Fort Apache* showing the womenfolk engaged in their domestic duties. Women, in most Ford Westerns, are set firmly within the family structure—a portrayal not likely to endear the director to militant feminists, but one necessary to the reconstruction of a *Gemeinschaft* social organization. Such a community ordinarily depends for its essential solidarity on close family ties. It is also defined by manners and customs (often involving "sex roles"), ceremonies and rituals that are conventional in origin but over the course of time acquire the force of unwritten law. In *Fort Apache*—and elsewhere in his work, one thinks of *My Darling Clementine* (1946)—Ford conveys this feeling for tradition and ritual by means of formal dances. (The choreographer who worked on the set of *Fort Apache* was certainly not extraneous to the director's purpose.) The cavalry itself is a prime element within the society; indeed it is the community's institutional *raison d'être*. The hierarchical structure of the military dovetails nicely with other parts of the *Gemeinschaft* community. As troublesome as it in many ways is, the ending of the film, as York leads his men outside the fort on their latest mission, establishes a sense of institutional continuity. Communal continuity is suggested by Philadelphia, now Mrs. Michael O'Rourke, who watches with her young son, Michael Thursday York O'Rourke, as the cavalrymen ride away. Questions about York (has he been transformed into another Thursday? has the pressure of command compromised his earlier integrity?) melt in the warm glow that emanates from Philadelphia's contented gaze. One of Ford's happier accomplishments in *Fort Apache*, then, is that he manages to convey the "feel" of an integral and fully functioning community.

Perhaps the most significant of the film's virtues, however, springs paradoxically from its most serious weakness. A root cause of Ford's ambivalent and sometimes confusing view of his subject is that in *Fort Apache*, for the first time in his work, he confronts Indian culture on its own terms; the Apaches are shown to be, not evil savages bent on thievery and killing, but human beings who have legitimate complaints against white society. Captain York respects Cochise, and the two men are able to deal with each other honestly and as equals; York genuinely hopes for a peaceful settlement of the dispute. He recognizes the validity of Cochise's grievances against the slimy and corrupt trader, Silas Meacham (Grant Withers). In the pre-battle conference between Cochise and Thursday, Cochise focuses his angry complaints on Meacham's acknowledged greed and dishonesty. Yet Thursday will not listen, and the battle takes place. If the Indians are not to blame, then who or what is? Obviously someone or something within the U.S. Military. One can almost visualize the director slowly but surely painting himself into a corner. Ultimately the only way he could escape his self-imposed entrapment was by means of a daring leap in logic—the thoroughly astonishing reversal at the end which, as I have indicated, fails to convince.

A decade earlier, in *Stagecoach*, Indians were unashamedly used as background props, the human obstacle that the cavalry had to surmount to prove its heroism and usefulness. Eight years after *Fort Apache*, Ford made *The Searchers* (also scripted by Frank Nugent[11]), his most complex and suggestive exploration of the "Indian question"—an exploration, it should be added, still conducted from the white's point of view.[12] In *The Searchers* the cavalrymen, in their brief appearance, no longer seem the knightly protectors of an embryonic society; their role now is clearly to enforce the principle of white supremacy. The Indian-hating Ethan Edwards (played superbly by John Wayne) unwittingly demonstrates that even heroic virtues can turn self-destructive when distorted by an obsessive desire for revenge. Ethan, consciously or subconsciously, senses his kinship to his adversary Chief Scar, but he cannot accept the implications of that kinship. Unable to soften his rigid code of conduct (even after sparing his niece), he assumes the burden of a terrible isolation; he becomes a version of "man alone," an individual who chooses to exist without the comfort or support of community and family.

The link between Ford's simplistic view of Indians in his earlier Westerns and his subtle and in many ways alarming examination of the impact of Indians (and their culture) on frontier whites in *The Searchers* is, I submit, *Fort Apache*. Indeed the importance of *Fort Apache* in this regard extends to a context much broader than one director's filmography. André Bazin says that *Fort Apache* marks "the beginning of political rehabilitation of the Indian" in the American cinema.[13] That is a claim some may want to challenge. But few would deny that the movie occupies a critical place in the development—as man and as artist—of its director, John Ford. Considering Ford's contributions to the Western film genre, that is glory and significance enough.

NOTES

1. RKO, 1948. John Ford and Merian C. Cooper, producers; Ford, director; screenplay by Frank S. Nugent, from the story "Massacre" by James Warner Bellah; Richard Hageman, music; Lucien Cailliet, music director; James Basevi, art director; Joe Kish, set director; Michael Meyers and Ann Peck, costumes; Emile La Vigne, makeup; Kenny Williams, choreography; Major Philip Keiffer and Katherine Spaatz, technical advisors; D. R. O. Hatswell, costume researcher; Frank Webster and Joseph Kane, sound; Dave Koehler, special effects; Archie Stout, camera; Jack Murray, editor.

2. *New York Times*, June 25, 1948, p. 26.

3. *Time*, May 10, 1948, pp. 102–104. Agee comments elsewhere that *Fort Apache* contains "enough Irish humor to make me wish Cromwell had done a more thorough job." See *Agee on Film* (New York: McDowell, Obolensky, 1958), p. 311.

4. James Robert Parish and Michael R. Pitts, *The Great Western Pictures* (Metuchen, New Jersey: Scarecrow Press, 1976), p. 102.

5. Russell Campbell, *"Fort Apache," Velvet Light Trap*, no. 17 (Winter 1977):12. The ending of *Fort Apache* is a much-discussed topic among critics of Ford's work. Perhaps the most spirited defense of the conclusion is offered by James McBride and Michael Wilmington in *John Ford* (London: Secker and Warburg, 1974), pp. 97–109. McBride and Wilmington's book is, on the whole, an excellent survey of Ford's pictures. Their discussion of *Fort Apache*, however, consists mostly of a series of unsupported assertions with which I cannot agree.

6. Agee, p. 311.

7. "I Come Ready," *Film Heritage* 10 (Summer 1975):4–5.

8. Quoted in Peter Bogdanovich, *John Ford*, rev. ed. (Berkeley: University of California Press, 1978), p. 86.

9. Quoted in Lindsay Anderson, "John Ford," *Cinema* 6 (Spring 1971):30.

10. Campbell, p. 9.

11. After Andrew Sarris released his late–1960s list of "Pantheon Directors"—which includes Ford—Richard Corliss did a half-serious, half-parodic takeoff on Sarris by constructing an "Acropolis of Screenwriters." Nugent is listed (seriously, I trust) among Corliss's top ten. See Richard Corliss, "The Hollywood Screenwriter," in *Film Theory and Criticism* (New York: Oxford University Press, 1974), p. 550.

12. *Cheyenne Autumn* (1964), which openly sympathizes with the Indians' cause, probably should at least be mentioned at this point; as a work of art, however, it is much less successful than *The Searchers*.

13. André Bazin, *What Is Cinema?*, vol. 2, trans. Hugh Gray (Berkeley: University of California Press, 1971), p. 151.

5

HIGH NOON (1952)

Don Graham

Don Graham is professor of English at the University of Texas at Austin. He is the author of The Fiction of Frank Norris: The Aesthetic Context *(1978).*

> clouds of half-regret
> on entering this genesis town
> a Gary Cooper showdown
>> Dave Oliphant, "Two Texas Poets Rendezvous
>> At The Bowie Public Library"

For many Americans, *High Noon* is *the* Western movie. The image of Gary Cooper peering through the broken window, his face lined with determination, or of Cooper turning on his heel, dropping his badge to the dust in weary disdain—such images are among the most enduring in American cinema. Yet there is scarcely a famous Western that has evoked more condescending or negative criticism than *High Noon*. Why this should be so and why at the same time the movie should continue to speak to us with great power are questions worth taking up.

Some critics think that *High Noon* adulterates the purity of the Western. It does this, they believe, in two ways: the addition of anachronistic social or political themes, or a confusion of styles. Robert Warshow represents the first point of view; he faults *High Noon* for its inclusion of a "social drama" that smacks of a "vulgar antipopulism."[1] What he means of course is the portrayal of the townspeople as hypocritical, self-serving, and cowardly. The technical result of including the social drama is to isolate the hero, to make him a man alone; but Warshow finds all of this unnecessary because in the traditional Western the hero was "naturally" alone.[2] Thus *High Noon* employs cumbersome devices to achieve what the traditional Western earned by its birthright. Warshow also dislikes the effect created by the hero at the end of the movie, an effect he labels "pathetic" rather than tragic.[3] Probably it would have been better if Cooper had died, as the hero of *The Gunfighter* does, a movie that Warshow considers truly tragic. But Cooper doesn't die, and nearly everything that Warshow says about the emotion generated at the end of *High Noon* seems wrong to me. The marshal is not, for example, a "rejected man of virtue" forced to leave the town; he chooses to leave the town.[4] The hypocritical well-wishers are there in the street, ready to thank him for doing what they were unwilling to help him do.

The second kind of objection to *High Noon* has to do with style. Auteur critics, who hold a particularly low opinion of *High Noon*, fault the movie for its combination of realism and something else—a stylization that takes the movie out of the context of history into myth.[5] Also, because they object to the history, they complain about that as well. Andrew Sarris sums up the kind of dislike I am talking about. Here is what he says of the gunfight in *High Noon:*

> If Zinnemann had wanted to sustain his realistic approach, he could have had Cooper mow his assailants down with a shotgun. Instead, *High Noon*, like most anti-Westerns, degenerates into a wasteful choreography of violent arabesques.[6]

In short, Cooper should have used a rifle as John Wayne did in *Stagecoach*. Here Sarris bases his criticism on two erroneous assumptions: that the Western must be true to history and that it must embody a single aesthetic mode. A necessary corrective attitude to hold if one is going to appreciate rather than dogmatize about Westerns is to realize that they are about ideas of the past (and present), rather than accurate reproductions of the past. Every time a strict notion of historical accuracy is introduced as a yardstick to measure the quality of a Western, the true nature of the form is overlooked. Thus *Stagecoach* is not *truer* than *High Noon;* both are versions of the past, one romantic and idealized, the other dark and constrictive. Moreover, *Stagecoach* does not need to establish the hero's puissance through "violent arabesques" because his skill and power have already been shown to be great indeed. In *High Noon*, though, some cathartic violence done in the old (movie) style is needful; up to this point at the end, we have scarcely seen Cooper in action. One is reminded of Sam Peckinpah's splendid re-creation of the heroic style in *Ride the High Country*. In the final climactic shoot-out, there are many practical ways to bring the outlaw family to justice, but the two aging heroes with, interestingly, the full cooperation of their adversaries, agree to do it in the old way, in the classic (and again movie) sequence of facing each other in a duel. I daresay that no audience who ever watched *High Noon* was not moved by the final and quite long showdown. Violent arabesques are sometimes aesthetically and emotionally right.

Although most essays on the Western mention *High Noon*, few go beyond praise or condemnation. Indeed I know of only one that is devoted entirely to *High Noon*, and it is a very unsatisfactory attempt to interpret the film as a modern-day version of the medieval play *Everyman*.[7] Other more significant interpretations have also focused on allegorical, non-Western elements. These are specifically political in nature. The first, set forth by a foreign critic, Harry Schein, sees *High Noon* as a symbolic explanation of U.S. foreign policy during the Cold War. In Schein's opinion Marshal Will Kane is America; the Frank Miller gang is the external threat posed by international Communism; Amy, Kane's new wife, represents isolationist sentiment within the nation; and the craven townspeople who refuse to help Kane are other nations content to let the U.S. go it alone in Korea to preserve world peace.[8] Aside from the interesting illogic of having Amy stand for an American isolationist while the townspeople—also Americans—stand for non-Americans, Schein's interpretation is an ingenious explanation of how some foreign observers saw *High Noon*. To see the film this way, in Sweden, say, in 1952, was certainly possible, but such a reading does not account for the movie's continued appeal to audiences born after the Cold War who associate Korea with a vague Congressional scandal if they associate it with anything at all.

A second allegorical interpretation locates the political meanings closer to home. According to this view, McCarthyism is the subject of *High Noon*. Will Kane recedes into secondary importance in this interpretation, with emphasis falling on the community turned cowardly by fear, commercial self-interest, and soft living. Carl Foreman, author of the script, has lent credence to this view.

In 1952, before the film was released, and in the wake of
Congressional hearings into alleged Communist activities in Hollywood, Foreman left the U.S. to dwell abroad. In an interview a few
years later he asserted that the movie was "an investigation of fear
as it affects the community rather than one individual."[9]

Unless prompted by film historians or cinema notes, an audience
today is not likely to find specific political meanings in *High Noon*.
Since the Korean War, America has fought another war that
seemed to invalidate the old formula of white hats versus black
hats. Further, invoking the specter of McCarthyism hardly has the
same effect now that it once did. Yet contemporary audiences do
respond to *High Noon*, and I think I know why. It is not because of
any political allegory, but because of other reasons. The first is the
desperate portrayal of anguish and lonely courage registered by
Gary Cooper's Will Kane. Critics who don't like the movie point to
the lack of authenticity of the Marshal's weakness. Cowboys didn't
cry, they maintain. My facetious reply is, How do you know? My
critical reply is: Kane breaks down (actually all he does is slump
over his desk, and I, for one, have never been able to *see* the tears
that some critics have reported) late in the movie, and then only
after he has been deserted by his young Quaker bride, the judge
who performed the marriage ceremony, the deputy marshal, a
citizen-friend who hides behind his wife's lie to keep from seeing
Kane, the former marshal, and a cross section of members of the
two most powerful institutions in the town, the church and the
saloon. To die for a town worth dying for is one thing; to die for a
bunch of backbiting hypocrites is something else. Finally, of course,
Kane is willing to die for himself, a commitment and risk that link
him, critics notwithstanding, to the heroic tradition of classic
Westerns. Moreover, what we remember most from the movie is
not the weakness but the will, not the moments of doubt but the
moments of action. And here is another reason why those violent
arabesques are justified.

If the hero of *High Noon* generates great emotional identification
with his heroism, the second direction of emotional power is one of
revulsion. The object of recoil is the townspeople, who for a variety
of reasons plead the necessity of their own non-involvement.
Depicting the townspeople in such fashion was something new in
Western movies. *High Noon* elevated the third and typically least
important element of a triad—hero, villain, townspeople—into
major importance.[10] Before *High Noon*, townspeople were a

lumpen composed of sodbusters, shopkeepers, and other nonde-
script types. They set in high relief the mobility and superior skills
of hero and villain, they talked about lynching prisoners and
sometimes did, they filled up saloons, they rushed about in clots,
and they were always there—in the background. *High Noon*
brought them front and center; it was not a pretty sight.

In making the townspeople contemptible and hypocritical, *High
Noon* vibrated a resonant chord; it tapped an American archetype
—the Hypocritical Community.[11] The dramatization of this archetype helps account for the continuing power of the movie, not its
now dated 1950s political implications. Something similar happens
in a famous science fiction film of the period, Don Siegel's *Invasion
of the Body Snatchers* (1957). This movie teases the viewer to take
an allegorical stance, to see the sinister threat of Communism
underlying the displacement of souls in mindless American citizens
by alien forces. Allegory aside, the movie is about anonymous
replication. So *High Noon*, allegorizing aside, is about hypocrisy. It
is a version of an archetype common in American literature, the
revolt against the village. Examples abound: E. W. Howe's *The
Story of a Country Town*, Sinclair Lewis's *Main Street*, Sherwood
Anderson's *Winesburg, Ohio*, and Larry McMurtry's *The Last
Picture Show*, each of which explores the price of individualism in a
tightly conformist and often destructively hypocritical society. The
relation of *High Noon* to this tradition is evident in its thematic
tensions, the conflict between Kane and his former friends, Judases
all, but most particularly in the name of Will Kane's town.

In John M. Cunningham's "The Tin Star," the story upon which
High Noon was based, the town where the sheriff lives is unnamed.
But in the movie the town bears a name as important as the change
from Sheriff Doane in the story to *Will* Kane in the movie. The
town's name does not impart a satirical Western flavor, such as
Shinbone in *The Man Who Shot Liberty Valance*, or a resonantly
regional image, such as Yellow Sky in Stephen Crane's famous
story. Instead the name sounds hardly prepossessing at all: Hadleyville. But it is: behind Hadleyville stands another small town in
American culture, Mark Twain's Hadleyburg. Visually the name is
featured several times: at the train station where Miller's gang
awaits his arrival, and on the Hadleyville Bank sign in the heart of
town. The closing gunfight takes place near the bank, with the sign
in prominent display.

Though not extensive, the similarities between *High Noon* and

"The Man That Corrupted Hadleyburg" are sufficient to establish a meaningful connection. Besides the echoic allusion in the name, another parallel is the calculated exposé of respectable members of the community wherein each figure—judge, church-going Christian, good neighbor, respectable businessman—has the mask of altruism stripped away to reveal baseness, greedy self-interest, fear. As in Twain's scathing satire on smalltown smugness and untested virtue, *High Noon* mocks and derides the mask of complacent morality. Before the mysterious stranger's visit to Hadleyburg, the town prided itself on being a community of decent people; afterwards, the citizens know in their hearts the degree of baseness of which each is capable. Their moral pretensions are in shreds. Before Frank Miller's return to Hadleyville, this town also thinks extremely well of itself. Afterwards, we don't know what the townspeople who hid behind their doors think, but we see them gathered around the haggard marshal and his brave bride, presumably to praise the couple for saving the town. But we do know what Will Kane thinks; he drops the tin star in the dust, and he and Amy leave town, their carriage speeding them briskly from a community that failed the man who had saved it five years before and who now has saved it again. Thus the conduct of the citizens of Hadleyville confirms the cynical castigation of the town by the judge as a "dirty little village in the middle of nowhere."

In its portrayal of village hypocrisy, *High Noon* is a somber movie indeed. Any elation we feel for Will Kane's success is always tempered by our responses to the community that he leaves. It is in this sense, then, that *High Noon* does have a political dimension. It is a movie about the relationship between a community and its leaders and thus political as an Elizabethan play about kingship is political. Like other noteworthy Westerns of the Fifties—*The Gunfighter, The Man From Laramie, The Left-Handed Gun*—*High Noon* is a study in generational conflicts.

In classic Westerns of the decade before *High Noon*, men were men. They might be strong men like the Ringo Kid in *Stagecoach* or weaklings like Peacock the whiskey salesman, but their status as adults was never at issue. Though one may think of exceptions—in talking about Westerns there are always exceptions—the generalization in the main holds: Westerns dealt with mature adults. One of John Ford's Cavalry movies illustrates the point well. *She Wore a Yellow Ribbon* (1949) presents the U.S. Cavalry as a microcosmic family stationed at an outpost of progress. The Father, Captain

Nathan Brittles (John Wayne), is beset with external problems—Indians, gunrunners—and internal ones—forced retirement,
transferring leadership to the junior officers. By solving all the
problems, *She Wore a Yellow Ribbon* affirms in a positive,
celebratory manner the transfer of authority and responsibility
from one generation to the next. The rising generation learns to
appreciate the values represented by the older, and there is no real
conflict, only a benign, firm guidance by the elders. In another
important Western of the Forties, Howard Hawks's *Red River*
(1948), the generational struggle is much stronger, a stormy,
frightening clash between a father turned tyrant and a "son" who is
potentially as good a leader as the father has been in the past. Like
Ford's, this film is secure in its belief that both generations have
their merits.

In the era of *High Noon*, however, things changed drastically.
For reasons too speculative to explore here, the issue of transfer of
authority from one generation to another became a matter of
disturbing uncertainties. In film after film in the 1950s there is no
young person worthy of assuming the responsibilities of adulthood.
Thus Westerns in this period express a view quite different from
what the youth-oriented movies were telling us. *Rebel Without a
Cause* and *The Blackboard Jungle*, for example, took the side of
youth, implying, according to one critic, that "only young people
had style and intelligence in a world where adults were characteristically drunk, dense, or vicious."[12] Westerns like *The Gunfighter*
and *High Noon* make the opposite point.

In *The Gunfighter* (1950) there are two generations: to one
belong men like Johnny Ringo (Gregory Peck), old at 35, a man
outside the law but nonetheless a man, mature, weary, responsible,
and his double, the sheriff Mark, who used to be outside the law but
is now its representative. Both men respect each other, and one,
Mark, holds the structure of the town together. Doomed by his
reputation, Ringo is not allowed to have a chance to lead, but it is
obvious that he could, and in fact in one comic scene he is mistaken
for a deputy by some irate ladies. The other generation is composed
of unworthy would-be gunfighters, or "young squirts" as the
dialogue insists upon their being called. In another type of Fifties
movie they would be called punks or hoods. They are stunted,
cocky, and stupid. One wonders where the next lawmen are going
to come from. The only hint of a possible succession of generations
is Ringo's son, a boy whom his mom, a schoolmarm, calls "wild but

good." In the one scene between them, Ringo teaches his son manners and holds up Mark as an ideal, a peace-keeper not a gunfighter. Whether the lesson takes or not, we never know. But the point throughout is that young pretenders to manhood are the threats to order, while the older generation possesses maturity and responsibility. In *The Gunfighter* no generation is waiting in the wings to take charge.

More bleak even than *The Gunfighter*, *High Noon* presents a crisis in the transfer of power, for it impugns both generations, fathers and sons. The judge who married Will Kane and Amy in an early scene appears to be a father figure. Kindly, benign-looking, he quickly reveals himself as a cynic interested only in self-expediency. When news of Frank Miller's release from prison reaches him, the judge packs his belongings and leaves town fast, telling Will that he "has no time for a civics lesson, my boy." But he does pause for a civics lesson, citing two historical precedents for towns surrendering their freedoms to returning tyrants, one drawn from classical history, the other from a Western setting eight years ago. Another possible father figure is the retired sheriff. He suffers from arthritic hands, an affliction that keeps him from helping the marshal, but in the interview with the older sheriff, the dominant underlying feeling is not physical disability but moral weakness.

Ironically, the person closest to being a true father figure is the one whom the judge calls "my boy": Will Kane. He is the father as groom, albeit an aged-looking one, especially in contrast to his young bride Amy (Grace Kelly). Part of the solitude of the marshal's condition derives from his generational loneliness. There is no one older than himself to turn to, and there is no one younger who is either capable of helping him or worthy of accepting delegated responsibility. Kane exists in the hiatus between a new marshal's arrival (due the next day) and the final hours of his own tenure of duty. The glimpses we see of the younger generations are not consoling. The only children in the film perform according to familiar genre conventions by parodying their elders' actions. Thus outside the church two groups of children play tug-of-war and both tumble to the ground; in another scene they play-act a gunfight, crying "Bang, bang you're dead, Kane," as Will makes his rounds. The only adolescent in the film, it is true, does volunteer to help Will, but he is only fourteen and awkward to boot. Will has to refuse his help. At the end the youth pays tribute to Will's courage in a manner befitting the marshal's feelings: he has the carriage ready for Will and Amy to depart immediately following the gunfight.

The sub-plot involving Kane's deputy, Harvey Pell (played beautifully by the weak-chinned Lloyd Bridges), reveals the generation-successor motif most clearly. Passed over as replacement for the retiring marshal, Harv accuses Will of having spoken against him before the town council. Will denies it, but does agree with them that sometimes Harv acts "too young." Harv's girl friend, Helen Ramírez (Katy Jurado), underlines this judgment in a devastating way. Formerly Will's girl (and once Frank Miller's!), she has a good basis for comparing both men. She calls Harv a "nice boy" and tells him it takes more than broad shoulders to be a man. Her advice is simple: "Grow up." Her lack of faith in Harv is so strong that she leaves town because she knows that with Will dead, the town will die.

But it is impossible for Harv to grow up. Unlike Will Kane who can withstand everything, even the loss of his still unravished bride, Harv can't act without self-interest receiving its due. Petulant, aggrieved over his rebuff by the city "fathers," Harv offers to help only if Will insures his appointment to be Will's successor. Harv's self-interest underlines what is wrong with the general citizenry of Hadleyville. Civic duty has become a venal act for which one must be paid. The old sense of duty, of fulfilling the letter of a promise, means nothing now. Except to Will Kane, of course. Harv's last act is to try to stop the marshal from performing his duty. Screwing up his courage with whiskey and stung by a bartender's taunt that he is a "boy with a tin star," Harv first tries to persuade Will to leave town, then tries to force him. In the memorably choreographed fight in the stable, Harv is soundly beaten.

Critics who detected a political message in *High Noon* were right in the most general sense, but misguided in trying to assign too specific allegorical equivalencies. *High Noon* is political in the way that the genre is political, for it is about leadership, the community, the very idea of what a city is.[13] Unlike many Westerns that depict the founding of a city, *High Noon* probes the question of the survival of a city. In the classic Western, of which *Shane* (1953) is a useful model, the hero saves the nascent city, preserving it for a society of good folk and removing himself in the process. Thanks to his hardihood and courage, the city will prosper. In *High Noon* the city has been founded long enough to wane in its

prosperity and to seek new infusions of energy from "up North."
The leading spokesman for the business interests in the town,
played by Thomas Mitchell, is a cheerleader for "new businesses
and factories"; bad public relations—such as a shootout in the
streets—will scare away those investors, he argues decisively before
the church audience. Hadleyville is a stagnant city that is saved
again, but we must wonder for what. The hero leaves, but with no
elegiac regrets. The town he saved was not and is not worth saving.
It has not been redeemed.

The mythos that *High Noon* so skillfully realigned was to prove
one of the most durable models of replication and innovation in the
Western genre in the years ahead. More than a half-dozen notable
Westerns took their impetus from *High Noon,* either revising its
legend with a counter legend or filling in the basic outline with
new variations.[14] The most famous revisionist work specifically
aimed at *High Noon* was *Rio Bravo* (1959), directed by Howard
Hawks and starring John Wayne. Wayne in particular was offended
by what he considered the spineless, un-Western moral temporiz-
ing of *High Noon.*[15] With its strong code of professional bravery
and loyalty, *Rio Bravo* sought to repudiate the weakness exhibited
in *High Noon.*

Other less celebrated movies embellished the man-alone myth of
High Noon in interesting ways. One of the best is Delmer Daves's
3:10 To Yuma (1957), which amplifies two motifs of *High Noon*
—redemption and regeneration—into a study of moral growth. A
version of the Grail myth, *3:10 To Yuma* analyzes the progress of a
small rancher who undertakes a difficult job in order to make
enough money to buy water to save his drought-threatened land.[16]
Van Heflin is hired to escort a clever outlaw, Glenn Ford, to a train
station where he will board a train bound for the Yuma prison.
During their brief time together, Ford proves to be a cunning
temptor, using many arguments to persuade the poor rancher to let
him escape. Heflin refuses, even as a money offer mounts to $10,000
and as various allies melt away. As in *High Noon,* the rancher's wife
makes a personal appeal too. Finally, alone and without help,
Heflin delivers Ford to the train where, out of respect for Heflin's
courage and secure in the knowledge that he can escape from
Yuma prison, Ford saves him. The movie ends with a thunder-
shower, rain for the parched land, water that symbolizes the
regeneration of the hero. By contrast, the landscape of *High Noon*
remains a wasteland.

Another excellent Western closely indebted to *High Noon* is *Firecreek* (1968), with James Stewart as a small rancher-father and Henry Fonda as a hardened outlaw. Fonda's gang, which contains some extremely vicious members, happens upon Firecreek, a withered town whose chief figures are an old, impotent cynic, a warm-hearted retarded youth, and a careridden ex-saloon girl. The gang soon has the town terrified, and its citizens prevail upon Stewart, who is also nominally the sheriff, to save them. Harried by family pressures—his wife is about to deliver a baby—Stewart temporizes until forced to realize that the threat offered by the gang has to be met head-on if the town—and its sheriff—is ever to have any self-respect. In a duel highly reminiscent of *High Noon*, Stewart defeats the gang, all but the leader who shoots him several times before he himself is felled by the saloon girl whom he has fallen half in love with. Both *3:10 To Yuma* and *Firecreek* express the positive, regenerative aspects of the *High Noon* pattern. In each the community is at least partially redeemed.

One *High Noon*-style Western that outdoes its predecessor in contempt for the community is Clint Eastwood's *High Plains Drifter* (1973), an innovative Gothic Western. *High Plains Drifter* dramatizes the revenge taken against a town for its craven desertion of its marshal, who some time in the past was whipped to death in the streets of Lago while the citizenry cowered behind doors. The avenger's identity is deliberately left ambiguous; he may be a brother, or he may be the ghostly spirit of the slain man. In any case there is certainly nothing ambiguous about his revenge: he sleeps with a prominent man's wife, takes whatever goods he pleases from the stores, appoints a dwarf as mayor, and finally, before burning the town, has it painted red to show forth the hell of personal selfishness that it so clear is. Like *3:10 To Yuma* and *Firecreek*, *High Plains Drifter* enacts its ritualistic meaning in public view, in the streets of an American town. Such films are eloquent testimony to the continuing relevance of *High Noon* to American movies and, beyond, to America's worries about its communal life.

NOTES

1. "Movie Chronicle: The Westerner," in *The Immediate Experience* (Garden City: Doubleday & Company, 1962 [1954]), p. 149.

2. *Ibid.*

3. *Ibid.*

4. *Ibid.*

5. A noteworthy exception to critics who dislike the film is André Bazin, who said, "I am not one of those who turn up their noses at *High Noon.*" "The Evolution of the Western," in *What Is Cinema?*, vol. 2, trans. Hugh Gray (Berkeley: University of California Press, 1971), p. 152.

6. "The World of Howard Hawks," in *Focus on Howard Hawks,* ed. Joseph McBride (Englewood Cliffs, N.J.: Prentice-Hall, 1972), p. 58.

7. Howard A. Burton, "*High Noon:* Everyman Rides Again," *Quarterly of Film Radio and Television* 8 (Fall 1953–54):80–86. This brief essay is filled with unconvincing parallels between the film and the play. One example: Cousin, a minor character in the play, has a sore toe; this is supposed to be an analogue for the retired sheriff's arthritic hands. For a more general discussion of parallels with *Everyman,* see George M. Hendricks, "Classical and Literary Motifs in TV and Movie Westerns," *Hunters & Healers: Folklore Types & Topics,* ed. Wilson D. Hudson (Austin: Encino Press, 1971), 127–31.

8. "The Olympian Cowboy," trans. Ida M. Alcock, *American Scholar* 24 (Summer 1955):316.

9. "An Interview with Carl Foreman," *Sight and Sound* (Summer 1958):220.

10. For a discussion of these character groupings, see John Cawelti, *The Six-Gun Mystique* (Bowling Green: The Bowling Green University Popular Press, 1971), pp. 47–52. My claim for *High Noon's* originality applies to sound movies; a notable silent precursor of the centrality of townspeople in a Western is William S. Hart's *Hell's Hinges* (1916). Even so, in this film the townspeople serve primarily an allegorical function; they are Sinners.

11. Ibsen's *An Enemy of the People* and Flaubert's *Madame Bovary* are useful reminders that American literature does not have a monopoly on this theme.

12. Andrew Dowdy, *The Films of the Fifties: The American State of Mind* (New York: William Morrow and Company, 1973), p. 157.

13. In a brilliant analysis of a pure genre Western, *Warlock,* Frank D. McConnell argues that "the hidden theme of the Western [is] the description of the origin of the city, of a civilized mass of human beings, with individualities defined only in a secondary relationship to that fundamental idea of the human crowd." *The Spoken Seen* (Baltimore: Johns Hopkins University Press, 1975), p. 153.

14. George N. Fenin and William K. Everson discuss the influence of *High Noon* upon such movies as *At Gunpoint!* and *Star in the Dust. High Noon* itself they rate as "inauthentic, too 'modern.'" *The Western: From Silents to the Seventies,* rev. ed. (New York: Penguin Books, 1973), p. 335.

15. A summary of Wayne's objections may be found in Jon Tuska, *The Filming of the West* (Garden City: Doubleday, 1976), p. 542.

16. Philip French notes in passing that *3:10 To Yuma* represents "a complex working out of the Grail legend in the West." Philip French, *Westerns: Aspects of a Movie Genre* (New York: Viking Press, 1973), p. 60.

6

SHANE (1953) and HUD (1963)

James K. Folsom

James K. Folsom is professor of English at the University of Colorado, Boulder.

Jack Schaefer's *Shane* (1949) and Larry McMurtry's *Horseman, Pass By* (1961) are two significant works of Western fiction. Successful books both, they reappeared as equally successful motion pictures—the first under the same title (1953), the second as *Hud* (1963).[1] Both movies faithfully followed the specific plots and general intent of the novels, unlike so many films—*The Big Sky* and *The Wonderful Country,* to mention two other Western novels so adapted—that too often bear little resemblance to their fictional sources aside from the same title. The faithful rendering of the novel by the motion picture based upon it in these two instances is partially attributable to the fact that both books are involved with thematic concerns that lend themselves to film treatment. Again this distinguishes them from many film versions of successful novels, which often center upon nothing more profound than the anecdotal interest of bizarre historical incident; or depend on the popular success of a colorful or notorious character (such as most film biographies, as well as films about a quasi-fictional character such as *All The King's Men,* adapted from Robert Penn Warren's novel based upon the life of Huey Long); or often solely upon the commercial desire to capitalize on the instant popularity of a

James K. Folsom, *"Shane* and *Hud:* Two Stories in Search of a Medium," *Western Humanities Review* 24 (Autumn 1970). © 1970 by *Western Humanities Review.* Reprinted by permission of the publisher and author.

successful book. In both *Shane* and *Horseman, Pass By*, however, the author's intent was to show the coming of age of a boyhood hero, a standard theme in both literature and films about the American West. In both books too, the boyhood hero must choose his way of life from among the various models of adult behavior that he sees around him and that are represented by the various characters in the novels—a method of fictional presentation admirably adapted to film.

More specifically, *Shane* and *Horseman, Pass By* lend themselves to film adaptation if only because they are short and fairly simple books, both with straightforward plot lines and relatively few characters. They do not, therefore, present the director with difficult and often paradoxical decisions of how best to preserve the author's "intent" when changing a novel to a film: or of how best to use the different techniques of cinema to achieve ends similar to a novel; or of the most satisfactory way to preserve the general character of an author's work while changing his particular artistic means in order to make the transition from printed page to screen. And most important, both novels relieve the director of the almost insoluble problem of how best to preserve the spirit of a sprawling "epic" novel, despite the inevitable distortion that cutting large sections of a complex book to manageable proportions for film treatment will produce. In the adaptation of neither *Shane* nor *Horseman, Pass By* was the film director faced with the problem of eliminating a large number of elements peripheral to the main story—as was, say, the director of the film version of James Jones's *From Here to Eternity;* or of the elimination of myriad subplots as in Dostoevsky's *The Brothers Karamazov;* or of the total suppression of almost entirely non-visual chapters, like the cetology chapters of Melville's *Moby-Dick.* In general, then, whatever changes were made in the film version of the two Western novels under discussion can be attributed to the varying specific demands of two different media rather than to some larger esthetic necessity to change the particular details of a book in order to preserve its general character.

Yet the differing demands of the written and visual arts *did* force a number of changes upon the directors of these two films; and an analysis of the implications inherent in these changes may be the best way to discuss at least some of the differences between visual and written art forms—differences of which we are all aware, however we may gloss over them by referring offhandedly to films as "versions" of novels. Different versions they may be, but the differences are very important: after all, Goethe's *Faust* and Gounod's *Faust*, though from one point of view only different versions of the same story, have far fewer points of similarity than of difference. We all realize this, and nobody would pretend to criticize Gounod wholly from the esthetic perspective of Goethe, knowing full well that the operatic form demands certain changes even from a form as closely related to it as traditional drama. But the heresy persists that films can often best be understood, as well as esthetically evaluated, in terms of the accuracy with which they reflect the details of the fictional work on which they are allegedly based, and of which they are presumably faithful copies. Copies of books their film "versions" most certainly are not; they are more like translations, attempts to render the very personal and specific metaphors of one language into the equally personal metaphors of a second. And hopefully, analysis of the metaphors of each language will give some insight into the points of difference between them.

That the essential point of difference is not in the plot becomes clear when we examine *Shane,* a novel whose plot was faithfully followed in the translation to film. The scene of both novel and film is Wyoming in 1889, and the plot of each is a descant upon the well-worn Western theme of the conflict between the arrogant cattle baron who claims ownership of the range and the home-steaders with whom he disputes possession. Both the novel and the film open with the arrival on the scene of Shane, a stranger who is just passing through and who stops at the homestead of Joe Starrett, leader of the homesteaders. In both novel and film Shane is a man with a past, a paradoxical figure familiar to readers of all kinds of Westerns—the gunfighter who would like to leave his guns behind. Joe Starrett persuades Shane to stay in the valley, where the situation deteriorates when Fletcher the cattle baron decides to force the homesteaders out. The homesteaders, under Starrett's leadership, form a league for their own defense, and Fletcher retaliates by trying to drive Shane out of town. Shane beats up one of Fletcher's men, and in a rather incredible scene he and Starrett beat up five others, after which Fletcher imports another gunfighter named Stark Wilson to finish the job for good. Wilson provokes a homesteader into a gunfight and kills him, and after this he, Fletcher, and two cowboys come to Starrett's ranch where they try to break up the homesteaders' league through an unsuccessful attempt to buy off both Starrett and Shane. Ultimately, Shane has to face Wilson, whom he kills along with Fletcher, though he is himself badly injured in the gun battle; and at the end of the novel, as in the movie, he rides out of town as mysteriously as he came.

Particular changes between the book and the film are relatively few, and many of them are of specific rather than general significance. Among the most important of these specific changes is the fact that the statement of the conflict between the cattle baron and the homesteaders is insisted upon from the beginning of the film, while in the book it becomes of importance only relatively late. The reason is of interest, and perhaps not immediately evident. For in the book the characters of Joe Starrett and Shane can be roughed out through the retrospective memories of Bob Starrett, Joe's son and the narrator of the novel, while in the film the character of each man must be developed in terms not only of symbolic but of actual physical interaction between him and some other character who stands clearly as a foil to him. In the film, therefore, Fletcher—who very clearly represents values that are placed in specific opposition to those of Joe Starrett—is introduced early, while in the book he exists as a nebulous presence, mentioned but never seen, until the plot has gotten well under way. Similarly, Stark Wilson, Fletcher's hired gunfighter, who represents a set of values antithetical to Shane's, is introduced almost immediately in the film and placed in specific contrast to Shane.

The more interesting changes from novel to film, however, are those general ones that are almost entirely attributable to the differing demands of a verbal and visual medium. First of all, in the film it is impossible for the boyhood narrator to be the controlling consciousness of the action to the same degree as was possible in the novel. The narrator of the events of the novel, Bob Starrett can only be the observer of them in the film. Rather than representing the controlling point of view, then, Bob becomes in the film only one among many characters, and a relatively minor character at that. Moreover, Shane himself changes in the film from the moral exemplum he was in the retrospective memory of the novel's boyhood narrator. He becomes a major character, visualized externally through his relationships with other characters rather than internally through Bob's nostalgic reflections upon his significance. Shane, then, does become the real focal point of the film as well as the titular hero of the book; he is important in his own right as a character rather than as a walking complex of character traits which he logically remains in the novel.

For its need to define Shane and Joe Starrett in terms of visually acceptable opposites, the film version of *Shane* must pay a certain price in complexity. One important area of conflict in the novel is almost totally eliminated from the film—the problem of whether Bob's mother, Marian, should stay with Joe Starrett or follow Shane, with whom she is obviously infatuated. An unintegrated and relatively disappointing aspect of both novel and film, its presence in the book can be tolerated—if not exactly welcomed—because the retrospective point of view of Bob Starrett implies no necessary opposition between Shane and Joe Starrett, however much there must have been in fact and—more important—*must* be visually if the conflict is to be shown at all on the screen. In short, Bob Starrett's memory of both Shane and his father as good men simply will not work so straightforwardly in a film: for inevitably the conflict between the two, when seen rather than remembered, implies some sort of moral opposition, thus destroying the neat pattern of polarities in which each positive character has his negative foil in the evil gunfighter and the rapacious cattleman.

Briefly, the retrospective quality of the novel cannot be insisted upon quite so obviously in the film. While we will accept the conflict in the novel as a remembered conflict told us much later by a boyhood observer now himself arrived at maturity, we must accept the conflict in the film as happening in the immediate present, and watch the education of the youthful Bob Starrett taking place under our very eyes. Moreover, Bob in his film role as one among many characters cannot comment upon the meaning of the unfolding action as he could in the novel. In the film he must live through the experiences that he remembers in the novel.

Another important difference between novel and film is related to this same point. For the need to conceive the conflict in the film as immediate, as happening directly before our eyes, implies that we must be able to visualize the characters. In fact, however, much of the stylistic power inherent in the novel *Shane* depends upon the opposite need that one *not* see the people Bob Starrett remembers. Just as the novel's focus is retrospective, so are its characters not so much concrete human beings as memories, subjectively conceived, which are summoned up only before the mind's eye: the characters, and most particularly Shane himself, do not really appear in the novel in their own right but rather as subjectively recalled creations of the mind of the nostalgic narrator.

This personal view becomes clear upon examination of some of the written descriptions of Shane. When in the novel he first appears at the Starrett ranch, Bob describes him in terms purposely both vague and general. What impresses Bob is the fact that the "newness" is gone from Shane's clothes, "yet a kind of magnificence" remains, accompanied by "a hint of men and manners alien to my limited boy's experience."[2] Much later in the novel, when Shane rides into town to face down Fletcher and Wilson, Bob describes him once more, and again the physical description of the man fades into its connotative associations. Now that he is no longer dressed in his farmer's clothes, Bob thinks, "he seemed again slender, almost slight," as he had when he had first ridden up to the Starrett ranch. Yet the change is seen primarily not in terms of observed physical appearance but rather of metaphorical descriptive connotations. "What had been seeming iron was again steel," Bob goes on. "The slenderness was that of a tempered blade and a razor edge was there." There is, a little later, "a catlike certainty in his every movement, a silent, inevitable deadliness," and as he rides off to face Wilson he is "tall and terrible there in the road, looming up gigantic in the mystic half-light"—not a man but a clearly visualized "symbol of all the dim, formless imaginings of danger and terror in the untested realm of human understanding."

Admittedly all this is a bit overdone, yet its purpose is clear enough. Schaefer hopes, through insistence upon these basically connotative descriptions, to make each reader build his own mental picture of Shane, who becomes visualized then not in actuality upon an external stage but retrospectively upon the internal landscape of the reader's mind. And this is an end which simply cannot be achieved in a film, where a character must be seen clearly in external terms.[3]

Schaefer's insistence upon this kind of retrospective and basically internalized description affects the action of the novel as well as the physical presentation of his characters. Since Shane himself is clearly stated to be a symbol of some of the formless aspects of the human spirit, his actions in the novel take on a moral and symbolic quality beyond their practical purpose. A clear example is a central symbolic scene of both novel and film in which Shane and Joe Starrett work together to pull a huge stump out of the ground. Just before the final effort Bob reflects that Shane is almost *willing* the stump out of the earth, and that his effort is at least as much a concentrated act of mental power as it is of physical force. Bob sees that "all of him, the whole man," is "pulsing" in an "incredible surge of power," noting that "you could fairly feel the fierce energy suddenly burning in him, pouring through him." Again this is acceptable, if somewhat overdone, as a fictional statement, especially in a novel in which we have been asked to create our own mental picture of Shane. But when one has to visualize the scene as it really happened rather than as someone remembers it, its entire character changes. Shane and Joe Starrett become merely two men prosaically sweating and tugging at a large stump in a field.

A similar difference in mood may be found in two of Shane's attributes, his horse and his clothes, both of which were changed —somewhat to the detriment of the film—from their novelistic source. Shane's horse, "moving with a quiet sureness and power that made you think of Shane himself," is clearly an extension of his rider, or better, an embodiment of the power and ominousness Shane represents to the narrator of the novel looking back upon his childhood through the mists of years. The point is clearly made when Shane calls the animal before riding off to face Fletcher and Wilson: "and the horse came out of the shadows at the far end of the pasture, its hooves making no noise in the deep grass, a dark and powerful shape etched in the moonlight." Esthetically, the description of the horse is more pleasing than the vague sketches of Shane himself; but the horse is just as difficult to visualize as his master, and for precisely the same reason: he is not a flesh-and-blood horse but a metaphorical statement of the ominous quality of "horseness," in precisely the same way that Shane is not himself so much a character as a symbolic statement of the "formless imaginings of danger and terror" in the human spirit.

Clearly such a horse cannot be found, and any attempt to place him on the screen is, almost by definition, doomed to failure. In fact the horse ridden by Shane in the film was a very nice horse, a bright chestnut with four white stockings and a comfortable single-foot road gait, but he impressed me more as an ideal child's horse than as a suitable mount for a man like Shane. The point, of course, is that *no* animal could have been a suitable mount for a man like Shane, since Shane's horse is not an animal of flesh and blood but a symbol.

Ironically, the other great change in Shane's attributes from novel to film—the change in the clothing of the motion picture

Shane—is also a visual change, and results in one of the few points of real difference in intent between film and novel. In the novel, what first impresses Bob about Shane is "his clothes." He wears "dark trousers . . . tucked into tall boots . . . of a soft black leather," and "a coat of the same dark material as the trousers." He has a kerchief of "black silk" knotted around his neck and wears a "plain black" hat—"unlike any hat" Bob "had ever seen." The important things about Shane's clothes are their strangeness and their dark color, both of which suggest the strangeness and intangibility of Shane himself. In the film, however, Shane wears a fringed buckskin shirt, and the effect of ominousness is almost totally lost, since Shane's clothes impress us not so much as those of a stranger as merely the work clothes of a character in another line of work. Just as farmers wear overalls, we feel, so do mountain men wear buckskins, and that is about the end of it.

The difficulty, of course, is again a visual one, for it is very hard indeed to present a character as ominous as the Shane of the novel upon the screen without his becoming threatening. In the novel we will accept Shane as powerful but benevolent because Bob—who presumably knows—tells us so; but when we actually have to *see* him as he is rather than as he is seen through Bob's prejudiced memories, his ominousness inevitably implies, at least in visual terms, a certain malevolence. And the point is clearly, if unintentionally, made through the figure of Fletcher's gunfighter Stark Wilson, a character more important in the film than in the novel, whose clothing in the film is precisely that of Shane in the book. Dressed totally in black and moving in a stylized fashion suggestive of his role as a symbol rather than a character of flesh and blood, the film Wilson (brilliantly played by Jack Palance) actually conveys many of the intangible qualities with which the novel endows Shane. In short, the complex of characteristics that the author of the novel can attribute to the benevolent Shane inevitably implies, when visualized, the malevolent Stark Wilson. Jack Schaefer, in sum, is able by controlling the implications of his retrospective point of view, to impute certain qualities to Shane's character which, when seen, must appear as basically contradictory.

The different treatments of the same story in the novel *Horseman, Pass By* and the film *Hud* also show clearly the difficulty of translating the "mood" of a work of fiction into film and the necessity imposed by a visual medium of having characters act as visible foils to each other. Once again the film closely follows the plot of the novel, both in specific incident and in general intent.[4] *Horseman, Pass By,* as *Shane,* is remembered in retrospect through the eyes of Lonnie, its now older boyhood observer, who reflects upon the significance of a series of events that had happened on the ranch of his grandfather, Homer Bannon. Homer, a man past eighty years old, his wife, and Hud, her son by a former marriage, live on a ranch in Texas together with Lonnie and Halmea, the black cook and housekeeper. At the beginning of the novel a dead heifer has been discovered that turns out to be a victim of hoof-and-mouth disease. Homer's cattle must all be destroyed in order to halt the spread of the disease, and the reactions of the characters in the novel to the worst disaster which can strike a cattleman, form both the conflict in the novel's plot and the catalyst for Lonnie's transition to adulthood.

In a sense the differences between the two treatments of the story are indicated by the change in title from *Horseman, Pass By* to *Hud.* Specifically, of course, the novel's title is a direct reference to the self-epitaph with which Yeats concludes his poem "Under Ben Bulben"—an epitaph also fitting to Homer Bannon. The title is generally relevant too, especially to the fifth section of "Under Ben Bulben," in which Yeats exhorts the Irish poets to celebrate native Irish themes rather than conventionally genteel ones, and more specifically, "well made" themes of "other days," of "heroic centuries" now past. Something like this feeling is basic to the thematic structure of *Horseman, Pass By,* which is, as a recent critic perceptively points out, a historic study of "the evolution of the Southwest . . . embodied in . . . three central characters," all of whom turn out to be different aspects of the "single image of the cowboy"[5]—a figure which itself exists in an uncomfortable and inconsistent world composed partly of myth and partly of reality. The point is nicely emphasized through the name of the town near which the Bannon ranch is located and where much of the novel's action takes place. For the town is named "Thalia" after the Greek muse of history and epic poetry.

This ambiguity inherent in the nature of "the West"—that part of the American experience that we like, conventionally at least, to think of as having epic potentialities—has been seen by many of the critics of the West as one important reason for the failure of Western themes to produce a literature of epic proportions. The West, it is alleged, is simply too close to us in historic terms to be viewed from what is conventionally considered to be an epic perspective; the prosaic reality of the cowboy's life intrudes involuntarily upon the mythic grandeur of the epic story. Whether this objection is ultimately true is beside the point here, but it does point up one factor in the "epic of the West" of which McMurtry is cognizant and of which in *Horseman, Pass By* he makes considerable esthetic use. For, to oversimplify, the adult world toward which Lonnie yearns at the beginning of the story he conceives in essentially heroic terms, a perspective that his experience ultimately teaches him is a false and childish one. Neither Hud nor Homer, however each may appear to the childhood observer, is wholly a walking embodiment of mythical characteristics. Both are characters of flesh and blood, with problems conceived of in human rather than epic terms.

The film's difference from the novel, to return, is nicely exemplified by the change in title. For the motion picture concerns itself with Hud in a way the novel does not, Hud becoming if not the film's moral hero very definitely its focal character. Again the film has had to make specific the various generalized aspects of the novel's "single image" of the cowboy and to present them in terms of direct foils. Hence the values that in the novel are scattered among a number of characters, in the film are polarized between Hud and Homer Bannon, both of whom come to represent two distinct and mutually exclusive models for adult life. Rather than having a general view of the adult world as presented retrospectively through a number of characters, the film Lonnie must make a specific choice between two models who are conceived of as being directly opposed to one another. Though at the beginning Hud seems to Lonnie more attractive, by the end of the film Homer has replaced him as the desirable model.

This overly schematic analysis of *Hud* may give the quite erroneous impression that it is less subtle than *Horseman, Pass By*. Such is most emphatically not the case. The difference is rather, that in the film subtlety is expressed through the nuances of conflict between the two major characters, Hud and Homer, while in the novel subtlety is expressed through proliferation of characters and—as in the novel *Shane*—through the retrospective musings of Lonnie himself upon the meaning of his own experience.

Horseman, Pass By is quite consciously conceived of as a mood piece, and McMurtry does a brilliantly effective job of presenting, through Lonnie's thought, the inchoate but very real yearnings of adolescence for something, it knows not what. In *Horseman, Pass By*, then, Lonnie's adolescent perspective may effectively be presented in terms of his yearnings for some kind of escape from the world in which he finds himself.

Although it is immediately clear what Lonnie wishes to escape *from*, it is not at all evident exactly what he wishes to escape *to;* nor in fact does he himself know. He expresses his yearnings in terms of sex and travel, two generalized metaphors which he sees embodied respectively in the figures of the cook Halmea and Jesse, one of the ranch hands. Quite the opposite is true of the symbolic pattern of *Hud*, in which, if only because we must see both Homer and Hud, we understand very clearly what Lonnie is drawn *toward*, and not so clearly what exactly he is reacting *against*. The respective endings of novel and film emphasize the point: for while the metaphor of the novel is of escape, that of the film becomes exile.

Again, the very real difference between the two versions of the story may best be seen by analyzing some of the changes from the novel made in the film. First of all is the fact that Halmea is changed in *Hud* from a black to a white woman, and Hud's rape of her, successful in *Horseman, Pass By*, is abortive in the film. Though this change originally may well have been prompted by non-esthetic considerations, it is nevertheless an effective one. The rape of Halmea in the novel is accomplished by Hud while Lonnie, who loves her, stands passively by. Though thematically this may make good sense, it is impossible to visualize except upon the screen of retrospective memory. In the novel Lonnie can tell us that this is what happened, without further explanation, and we accept his statement, though not without some mental reservations. But when the scene is actually presented to us we withhold our assent. When we must actually see the scene rather than having it reported to us, the basic improbability of the action becomes evident.

A more important change in the film is in the development of Hud's character. In the novel Hud's attractiveness to Lonnie as an image of successful sexuality is not really insisted upon until the rape of Halmea, while in the film this aspect of Hud's character is emphasized from the beginning. Early in *Hud* Lonnie is seen searching for Hud, whom he finds in the house of a married woman whose husband is away. The adolescent devil-may-care attractiveness of Hud to Lonnie is clear in this scene, which stands in

clear symbolic contrast to the unattractive aspect of the same side
of Hud as presented through the attempted rape of Halmea. In
Horseman, Pass By the contrast can be, and is, more abstract.

The necessity in the film to place Hud and Homer Bannon in
direct contrast issues into one other really major change, the almost
total omission of Jesse, the ranch hand. In *Hud* Jesse's role is
reduced to that of a walk-on part, while in *Horseman, Pass By* he is
a major character.

The reason behind the change is again visual. In the novel both
Hud and Jesse act as direct comparisons to Homer. Hud's morality
is placed in specific contrast to Homer's, in both novel and film, in
terms of the two men's different reactions to the discovery of
hoof-and-mouth disease in their cattle. After the initial shock has
worn off, Homer realizes that the only moral choice open to him is
to have his cattle slaughtered, and he accepts the necessity for the
destruction of his entire herd. Hud, in contrast, proposes to Homer
that they sell the cattle before the disease is diagnosed and the herd
quarantined. If someone is "stupid enough to buy" the cattle, Hud
sees no objection to selling them. In short, *caveat emptor.* "That
ain't no way to get out of a tight," Homer says, and refuses.[6]

Jesse, in contrast, acts as a foil to Homer in terms of the theme of
escape. For he has been everywhere, Lonnie thinks, and Lonnie's
own yearnings for distant places are gratified by listening to Jesse
talk of his experiences "on the rodeo circuit." "Just hearing the
names," Lonnie says, "was enough to make me restless."

Hud eliminates the theme of Lonnie's yearnings for escape that
is central to *Horseman, Pass By,* and therefore of necessity
decreases Jesse's significance and eliminates the minor subplot of
the Thalia rodeo and Jesse's failure to perform creditably at it. The
need inherent in a visual medium to establish an explicit polarity
between Hud and Homer is again the explanation. While in the
novel both Hud and Jesse may act as contrasts to different aspects
of Homer, in the film the distinction between Hud and Jesse must
inevitably be blurred because of the fact that since Homer must be
visualized as a person they must be seen in contrast to all of him
rather than to specifically differentiated qualities of his character.
Therefore Hud and Jesse, had they remained of equal importance
in the film, would inevitably have become redundant rather than
complements to each other. The difference between them, in short,
which is of basic importance to the novel, would have appeared

less striking on the screen than their overpowering similarity in terms of their not being Homer.

This point is perhaps best illustrated by a scene from the novel that was carried into the film almost intact. In both *Hud* and *Horseman, Pass By,* Homer keeps on his ranch three longhorn cattle in addition to his beef herd as a reminder of the old days. "Cattle like them make me feel like I'm in the cattle business," he says. These three longhorns must be destroyed with the rest of the herd, since they too are presumably infected with hoof-and-mouth disease.

In the novel, when the longhorns are being rounded up Jesse suggests to Homer that he let them go. "If the government wants 'em, let the government go find 'em," he says. Homer brushes off the suggestion by saying, "I don't know what to think yet"; but when the diagnosis of hoof-and-mouth disease is confirmed he has these cattle killed along with the others. In the film, significantly, the suggestion to Homer is made not by Jesse but by Lonnie, and his remark to his grandfather that the longhorns ought to be let go is very clearly reminiscent of Hud, who has made almost exactly the same suggestion about how best to get rid of the infected herd. Again, the film has concentrated its effect rather than spreading it out over a number of characters, since visually the most important thing is not which particular character makes the suggestion but that the suggestion itself is one totally antithetical to Homer's own values. In the film Lonnie has received a direct lesson in terms of two diametrically opposed characters; in the novel, by contrast, the same opposition can be expressed without redundance by more than one character, if only because each character, if not seen, is visualized by the reader as representative of a more or less isolated point of view rather than as a person of flesh and blood, someone who stands in opposition to relatively specific qualities in Homer Bannon rather than to his entire character.

This necessity to condense all the foils to Homer in the character of Hud inevitably implies the one major change between novel and film—a total reversal of the ending. Lonnie learns, through the action of *Horseman, Pass By,* the futility of his own generalized longings for escape. The world, he discovers, when viewed with, in Yeats's phrase, "a cold eye," is not the romantic place he had thought it was at the beginning of the novel. Captive at the beginning of the story of the common adolescent belief that

somewhere there must be more "life" than there is in one's own
environment, Lonnie learns the truth symbolized by the name of
the town—Thalia—where the story's action has taken place: that
the stuff of life and history and epic poetry must be discovered in
one's own surroundings if one has the intelligence to know where to
look for it.

In the novel, then, Lonnie's education culminates in his acceptance of the world for what it is and his rejection of the unreal
attitudes toward it he had held at the beginning of the story. In the
novel's final scene, after Homer's death, Lonnie hitches a ride on a
truck to visit a friend injured in the Thalia rodeo and taken to the
hospital at Wichita Falls. For a while, Lonnie says, "I was tempted
to do like Jesse once said: to lean back and let the truck take me as
far as it was going." But his newly achieved maturity enables him
to reject this temptation, and he decides to stop at Wichita Falls,
see his friend, and then return to Thalia.

In *Hud* the ending is quite different. Here, Lonnie's newly won
maturity has taught him not to accept the world as it is, but rather
to see the validity of Homer's attitude toward life and to reject the
tempting but ultimately immoral standpoint represented by Hud.
Lonnie has, therefore, no choice but to leave the world dominated
by Hud that the Bannon ranch has become after Homer's death;
and so at the end of the film he sets out to make his own way in the
great world he has rejected in the novel. While the ending of
Horseman, Pass By showed Lonnie's new maturity by emphasizing
his realization of the flimsiness of his adolescent longings for
escape, the ending of *Hud* shows it in terms of his symbolic
acceptance of Homer's attitude toward the world and his rejection
of Hud's.

The major differences between the stories of Shane and Hud as
they are presented on film or on the printed page are largely
implicit in the very different points of view required by the two
media. The primacy of vision in the film, though perhaps an
obvious point, cannot be too strongly insisted upon. It results first of
all in the necessity for an almost complete denial of both the
retrospective mood and the nostalgic point of view upon which the
fictional versions of both stories heavily rely. The internalization of
the fictional point of view implied by the reminiscences of an older
hero reflecting upon his past is simply impossible to achieve with
either success or consistency upon film for two reasons: first of all,
the narrator of the novel must inevitably become one among many

characters in the film; and secondly, the action of the story when seen must be seen as occurring in the present.[7]

An equally important, and less obvious, difference between novel and film also follows from the primacy of vision implied by the latter. For although the phrase "cast of thousands" has become a cliché for describing the so-called "epic" film, in fact the necessity for externalization implicit in the film results in an overwhelming tendency to simplify by reducing the number of characters. Most of the cast of thousands are background characters whose function is analogous to the consciously generalized mood-painting used by the novelist as a way of establishing his setting.

For all their specific differences, however, both media have in common one basic attitude toward their material—an attitude that has been present in Americans' treatment of their epic since the West was first assumed to be the most significant factor in the American experience and the unique part of that experience which set it off from other lands and other peoples. This attitude comes ultimately from an environmentalist belief, inherent in primitivism, that man reflects in moral terms the physical nature of his environment. This belief, which is in fact nothing more than an assumption, is treated as though it were axiomatic for interpreting the materials of the great American epic. Whether, as with Natty Bumppo, the American hero directly reflects the glory of his environment or, as with Emerson's strictures upon New Hampshire, the comment that "The God who made New Hampshire/ Taunted the lofty land/With little men" is ironic,[8] the importance of the analogy is never doubted. And the Western film has absorbed this analogical comparison between man and his environment. In the film, Shane has picked up, along with his other attributes, the quality of a mountain spirit, representative of the brooding grandeur of the Grand Tetons against which he is filmed, an analogy specifically evoked by the mountain man's buckskin shirt he wears and by the theme song of the film, "The Call of the Faraway Hills." In *Hud* the analogue is more ironic, but the bleak Texas landscape, the stark ranchhouse on the Bannon ranch, and the ugly town of Thalia make much the same symbolic point: for Hud expresses them exactly as Shane expresses the mountains.

The great problem, then, shared by both the Western film and Western fiction is the problem of presenting man against the landscape. What is the landscape, first of all: the beauty of the Grand Tetons or the ugliness of the Bannon ranch? And how does man stand against it: does he stand *for* it, symbolizing in detail what it expresses in general? or does he stand *in contrast to* it, repudiating everything it represents? There are of course no simple answers to these questions, all expressions of a basic ambiguity in the American identity; no answers, that is, except for the statement of the metaphorical problem and of its ritual solution.

NOTES

1. The change in the latter's title was a decision made by Paramount Studios. See Larry McMurtry, *In a Narrow Grave: Essays on Texas* (Austin: The Encino Press, 1968), pp. 4 ff. for details. The final title *Hud* is a shortened form of Paramount's working title, *Hud Bannon against the World.*

2. *Shane* (Boston: Houghton Mifflin Company, 1949). All further references are to this edition.

3. The interested reader who does not remember the film may test my point by searching out one of the illustrated editions of the novel and noting how different the pictures of both characters and events are from his own mental conceptions of them.

4. Indeed McMurtry, who praises *Hud* at the expense of *Horseman, Pass By,* sees the weakness of the film in its too great faithfulness to the novel. See McMurtry, *In a Narrow Grave,* p. 17.

5. Thomas Landess, *Larry McMurtry* (Austin: Steck-Vaughn Company, 1969), pp. 10, 14. Landess's study of McMurtry is generally excellent, though his interpretation of certain aspects of *Horseman, Pass By*—notably the ending—differs from my own.

6. *Horseman, Pass By* (New York: Harper & Brothers, 1961). All further references are to this edition.

7. This is true, I think, even of films—unlike these two—that use technical variations of the flashback as ways of insisting upon a film's action having happened in the past. Such action, even when we are assured by such violations of point of view that it did actually happen in the past, nonetheless seems to me to be happening in the present.

8. "Ode Inscribed to W. H. Channing," 11. 24–26.

7

RIO BRAVO (1959)

Robin Wood

Robin Wood teaches in the Fine Arts Department, York University, Toronto, Canada. He is the author of Howard Hawks *(1968).*

Rio Bravo is the most traditional of films. The whole of Howard Hawks is immediately behind it, and the whole tradition of the Western, and behind that is Hollywood itself. If I were asked to choose a film that would justify the existence of Hollywood, I think it would be *Rio Bravo*. Hawks is at his most completely personal and individual when his work is most firmly traditional: the more established the foundations, the freer he feels to be himself. Everything in *Rio Bravo* can be traced back to the Western tradition, yet everything in it is essential Hawks—every character, every situation, every sequence expresses him as surely as every detail in an Antonioni film expresses Antonioni.

List the stock types of Western convention, and your list will almost certainly include the following:

1. Hero: strong, silent, infallible.
2. Hero's friend: flawed, fallible, may let him down or betray him (through cowardice, avarice, etc.).
3. Woman of doubtful virtue, works or sings in saloon, gambles; will probably die saving hero's life.
4. Nice girl, schoolteacher or farmer's daughter, open-air type, public-spirited; will marry hero when he settles down.
5. Hero's comic assistant, talks too much, drinks.

Robin Wood, pp. 35–37 of *Howard Hawks* (Garden City, New York: Doubleday, 1968). © 1968 by the British Film Institute. Reprinted by permission of the British Film Institute.

6. Singing cowboy, plays guitar.
7. Comic Mexican, cowardly, talks too much, gesticulates.

In six of these seven stock types we can recognize the basis of the six leading characters of *Rio Bravo;* only the clean-living farmer's daughter is missing. These stock figures are used without the slightest self-consciousness or condescension. Hawks builds on these traditional foundations; he also builds on his actors, exploring and using their particular resources and limitations creatively. Here John Wayne, Dean Martin, Walter Brennan, and others are able to realize themselves, to fulfill the potentialities of their familiar screen *personae.* The extraordinary thing is that, while they can all be referred back to traditional Western types and to the personalities of the actors, the characters of *Rio Bravo* are at the same time entirely and quintessentially Hawksian, unmistakable in their behavior, their attitudes their dialogue. The film offers, I think, the most complete expression we have had of Hawks himself, the completest statement of his position. There are no clichés in *Rio Bravo.*

The complex flavor of the film can be partly defined in terms of apparent contradictions: it is strongly traditional yet absolutely personal; it is the most natural of Westerns, all the action and interrelationships developing organically from thematic germs that are themselves expressed as actions, yet it is also stylized; if one looks at it dispassionately, one becomes aware of an extreme austerity—a few characters, the barest of settings, no concessions to spectacle (with the exception of the dynamite at the end) or prettiness, yet if one submits to the atmosphere and "feel" of the film one is chiefly aware of great richness and warmth. These characteristics are all very closely interconnected. It is the traditional qualities of the Western that allow Hawks to make a film so stylized in which we are so little aware, until we stand back and think about it, of stylization; the stylization and the austerity are but two ways of naming the same thing; the richness and warmth emanate from Hawks's personality, which pervades the whole; and it is the traditional and stylized form that sets him free to express himself with the minimum of constraint or interference.

The term "traditional," applied to the Western, can mean two things, and two very different kinds of Western. The genre gives great scope to the director with a feeling for America's past, for the borderline of history and myth, the early stages of civilization,

primitive, precarious, and touching. But the genre also offers a
collection of convenient conventions which allow the director to
escape from the trammels of contemporary surface reality and the
demand for verisimilitude, and express certain fundamental human
urges or explore themes personal to him. If the classic Westerns of
John Ford, with their loving and nostalgic evocation of the past, are
the supreme examples of the first kind, *Rio Bravo* is the supreme
example of the second. The distinction, obvious enough yet very
important, can be exemplified by comparing the town in Ford's *My
Darling Clementine* with the town in *Rio Bravo*. Ford's Tombstone
is created in loving detail to convey precisely that sense of
primitive civilization against the vastness and impersonality of
nature, the profound respect for human endeavor and human
achievement exemplified in even the simplest of men that is so
characteristic of this director: on the one hand the Bon Ton
Tonsorial Parlor and honeysuckle-scented hair-spray, the tables in
rows neatly laid with cloths in the dim hotel dining-room; on the
other, the vast expanses of wilderness from which strange-shaped
rocky projections grandly rise. Ford places his community against
the wilderness, the wooden hotel, the skeletal church tower, the
dancers on the uncovered church floor unselfconsciously enjoying
themselves under the sky, surrounded on all sides by the vast
emptiness of the desert.

There is nothing like this in *Rio Bravo*. Here the whole Ford
theme of the defense of civilized order and civilized values against
destructive elements is compressed into the single strong reaction
evoked so powerfully by the murder, brutal, gratuitous, stupid, that
precipitates the entire action. Hawks's town consists of jail, hotel,
saloons, and rows of unadorned and inconspicuous housefronts;
inhabitants appear only when the narrative demands their presence, and there is never the least attempt to evoke that sense of
community that is one of the finest and most characteristic features
of the work of Ford. If a barn contains agricultural implements,
they are there to provide cover in a gun-fight, not to suggest a
background of agricultural activity; if the barn is littered with dust
and straw, this is not to create atmosphere or a sense of place, but
simply to use to blind a character momentarily. Every item of
decor is strictly functional to the action. The social background is
kept to the barest minimum below which we would be *aware* of
stylization. Even the jail and hotel which are the two main centers
of the action are not felt as having any real social function (no one

seems to stay in the hotel unless the plot requires them: mainly only Angie Dickinson); but there is a certain unobstrusive symbolic opposition between them (women tend to dominate in the hotel, and are excluded from the jail, where a miniature all-male society develops in isolation). The bar in which the action begins is so neutral in atmosphere that it scarcely registers on the spectator as a "presence": Hawks uses it neither to suggest any potential fineness of civilization (however primitive) nor to create a background of incipient violence and disorder; it is just a bar. Neither is there any attempt at "period" evocation: the costumes, while not obstrusively stylized, are quite neutral in effect.

The result of all this is twofold. It frees Hawks from all obligation to fulfill the demands of surface naturalism, the accumulated convention of the Western tradition allowing him the simplest of frameworks which can be taken on trust; and this enables him to concentrate attention on the characters and their relationships, and the characteristic attitudes and themes developed through those relationships, to an extent impossible in an outdoor Western: we feel far more intimate with the characters of *Rio Bravo* than with those of *Red River,* let alone *The Big Sky.* The neutral background of the opening scene throws the initial confrontation between Wayne and Martin into forceful relief. But it would be a mistake to see the stark simplicity of setting in this film as *merely* a convenience. It has also, and more importantly, an expressive function, providing a perfect environment for the stoicism that characterizes Hawks's attitude to life. The action of *Rio Bravo* is played out against a background hard and bare, with nothing to distract the individual from working out his essential relationship to life. The virtual removal of a social framework—the relegating of society to the function of a *pretext*—throws all the emphasis on the characters' sense of *self:* on their need to find a sense of purpose and meaning not through allegiance to any developing order, but within themselves, in their own instinctual needs.

The value of existing conventions is that they not only give you a firm basis to build on but arouse expectations in the spectator which can be creatively cheated. We can study this principle in any art form in any period where a highly developed tradition is available to the artist. One can see it very clearly in Mozart: much of the freshness of his music, its ability continually to surprise and stimulate the listener into new awareness, derives from his use of

the "conventional" language of the age in order to arouse and then
cheat expectations—from a constant tension between the conventional background and the actual notes written. The effect depends
very much on our awareness of the background, which needn't
necessarily be a *conscious* awareness. This tension between foreground and background, between the conventions of the Western
and what Hawks actually does with them, is everywhere apparent
in *Rio Bravo*. It will be immediately evident, for anyone who has
seen the film, in the relationship of the actual characters on whom
the film is built to the stereotypes I listed above. Consider, for
example, how Hawks uses John Wayne—both his qualities and his
limitations. He is the archetypal Western hero, strong, silent,
infallible. His taciturnity becomes the occasion for humor (especially in the scenes with Angie Dickinson) which is dependent
partly on our awareness of John T. Chance as a genre-character; at
the same time, the concept of stoical heroism Wayne embodies
provides the film with one of its major touchstones for behavior.
For all the sophistication and the unobtrusive but extreme virtu-
osity, Hawks's art here has affinities, in its unselfconsciousness, its
tendency to deal directly with basic human needs, its spontaneous-
intuitive freshness, with folk-song. Consider, for instance, the
refusal to identify most of the characters with anything beyond
descriptive-evocative nicknames: Dude, Feathers, Stumpy, Colorado . . . even Chance *sounds* like a nickname. Colorado has a
surname somewhere, but who remembers it? One feels the
characters as coming from a folk-ballad rather than from any actual
social context: they have that kind of relationship to reality.

Feathers is the product of the union of her basic "type"—the
saloon girl—and the Hawks woman, sturdy and independent yet
sensitive and vulnerable, the equal of any man yet not in the least
masculine. The tension between background (convention) and
foreground (actual character) is nowhere more evident. We are
very far here from the brash "entertainer" with a heart of gold who
dies (more often than not) stopping a bullet intended for the hero.
Angie Dickinson's marvelous performance gives us the perfect
embodiment of the Hawksian woman, intelligent, resilient, and
responsive. There is a continual sense of a woman who really grasps
what is important to her. One is struck by the beauty of the
character, the beauty of a living individual responding spon-
taneously to every situation from a secure center of self. It is not so
much a matter of characterization as the communication of a

life-quality (a much rarer thing). What one most loves about Hawks, finally, is the aliveness of so many of his people.

Stumpy (Walter Brennan) and Carlos (Pedro González-González) are brilliant variants of the Western's traditional "comic relief" stock types. Both are so completely integrated, not only in the action, but in the overall moral pattern, that the term "comic relief" is ludicrously inadequate to describe their function. With Stumpy, as with Chance/Wayne, the traditional figure merges indistinguishably into the personality of the actor. Brennan's *persona* of garrulous and toothless old cripple has been built up in numerous other films. Hawks's method with Brennan/Stumpy is the same as with Wayne/Chance: the character is pushed to an extreme that verges on parody. With Chance this has the effect of testing the validity of the values the *persona* embodies by exposing them to the possibility of ridicule. With Stumpy the effect is dual: on the one hand we have Brennan's funniest and richest, most completely realized impersonation; on the other, the character's position in the film ceases to be marginal (as "comic relief" suggests). His garrulity gradually reveals itself as a cover for fear and a sense of inadequacy; it plays an essential part in the development of the action, contributing to Dude's breakdown. With Stumpy, humor and pathos are inseparable. The response the characterization evokes is remarkably complex: he is funny, pathetic, maddening, often all at the same time; yet, fully aware of his limitations, we never cease to respect him.

Carlos raises a more general problem: what some critics have described as Hawks's racist tendencies. I feel myself that Hawks is entirely free of racial feeling; with Carlos, with the Dutchman in *Only Angels Have Wings*, with the French-Canadians in *The Big Sky*, he is simply taking over genre-figures (and often the character-actors associated with them) and building on them. One can say that the very existence of such stock figures is itself insulting, and this is fair enough; one can, I suppose, go on from that to complain that Hawks is unthinkingly helping to perpetuate the insult; but that is rather different from finding actual racial malice in his attitude. He is simply—and very characteristically—making use of the conventions (and the actors) that are at hand, and not questioning their initial validity. He takes the stock figure of the comic, cowardly, gesticulating, garrulous Mexican and, by eliminating the cowardliness while playing up the excitability, builds up a character whose dauntlessness and determination win our sympathy and respect even as we laugh at him. Hawks's handling not only revivifies and humanizes the stock type, but greatly increases his dignity and (moral!) stature.

But it is the figure of the Hero's Fallible Friend that is most fully worked on and transformed in *Rio Bravo.* Significantly, perhaps, this is the least stereotyped, the most uncertain and unpredictable, of the traditional Western ingredients. What I have in mind, however, is a character the variations on which the reader will have little difficulty in recognizing, whose function is usually to act as a foil to the hero, to set off his integrity and incorruptibility. Usually, he falls from grace either through weakness, personal inadequacy, or (more often perhaps) his betrayal of the hero, and gets killed. The characters played by Arthur Kennedy in two of Anthony Mann's excellent Westerns, *Where the River Bends* and *The Man from Laramie,* are interesting variants on the basic type; Lloyd Bridges in *High Noon* is another example. A part of his function—a foil to set off the hero's moral infallibility—is still clearly operative in *Rio Bravo;* but Dude takes on such importance in the film that it becomes a question at times who is a foil for whom. Hawks says *Rio Bravo* is really Dean Martin's picture; and if one disagrees, it's not because it's John Wayne's, but because what gives *Rio Bravo* its beauty is above all the interaction of all the parts, the sense that its significance arises from the ensemble, not from any individual character in isolation. Otherwise Hawks (who said of the ending of *Red River* that he couldn't see the sense of killing people off unnecessarily) exactly reverses the Fallible Friend's usual progress: instead of decline and betrayal, we have a movement (despite setbacks) towards salvation. And it is very important that the first step in that salvation is the mainspring of the film's whole action: it is typical of Hawks that everything should hang, ultimately, on a matter of *personal* responsibility, not social duty.

The wordless first minutes of the film are a good example of Hawks's use of actions to speak for themselves. Why does Dude strike Chance down? Why does Chance, despite his injury, so rashly—on the face of it hopelessly—follow and try to arrest Joe Burdett? Why does Dude help him? We feel we know the answers to all these questions, though they are never spelled out. All are essential to the film, and to what Hawks stands for.

The flooring of Chance establishes a basis on which Dude's whole development is built—his reluctance to be dragged up from the gutter when it is so much easier to sink further; and the resentment of the fallen man for the apparently infallible. Chance's single-handed attempt at arresting Joe Burdett in a saloon full of Joe's friends gives us a perfect image of the Hawks hero. There is no element of showing off nor of self-willed martyrdom: Chance's attitude is rooted in a personal need for self-respect, which demands that an action that must be done be done unquestioningly, without fuss, and alone, even in the teeth of hopeless odds. Dude's intervention sets the pattern for the whole film, where at every crisis Chance is saved by assistance he hasn't asked for or has rejected; but its motivation is equally fundamental to the spirit of the film. When Chance prevented Dude from taking the coin from the spittoon, Dude was made conscious of his degradation; his beating-up by Joe intensifies this consciousness. Above all, he is confronted by two opposite examples: the moral disintegration of Joe, the moral integrity of Chance. On his choice between them depends his salvation as a human being: his decision to help Chance (physically) commits him to an attempt to save himself (morally and spiritually). To express all this purely through simple physical actions is profoundly characteristic of Hawks; so is the immediately established positive trend of the character-development. There is nothing glib or sentimental about Hawks's treatment of his characters, but if he can possibly steer them towards salvation, he does.

If in *Rio Bravo* the traditional Western theme of the defense of civilized values is reduced to little more than a pretext, where, then, does Hawks put the emphasis? On values below the social level, but on which social values, if valid, must necessarily be built: man's innate need for self-respect and self-definition. As a motif, it will be easily seen that this pervades the film, as a unifying principle of composition. It is stated through virtually every character, usually on his first appearance, like the subject of a fugue, and developed throughout contrapuntally with fugal rigor. The film's first actions constitute a negative statement (Dude groveling for the coin in the spittoon) and a positive one (Chance's intervention, and the ensuing arrest of Joe Burdett). The first words of Colorado (Ricky Nelson) insist on his rights as an individual: when Chance questions Pat Wheeler (Ward Bond) about him in his presence, he interrupts with, "I speak English, Sheriff, you wanna ask me." Pat, too old and unsteady to be of direct use, risking (and giving) his life to get others to help Chance; Stumpy asserting his independence by disobeying Chance's orders and standing in the jail doorway; Feathers refusing to stop gambling and wearing feathers as a way of escaping a suspect past ("That's what I'd do if I were the kind of girl that you think I am"); Carlos insisting with sudden touching dignity on his right to arrange matters as he pleases in his own hotel: all these constitute variants on the theme. *Variants*, not repetitions: the statements range from broad humor (Stumpy) to near tragedy (Dude); each is distinct from the others in tone and in moral weight. Examples could be multiplied throughout the film. There is a continual sense of contrapuntal interaction of the various levels of seriousness and humor, so that great complexity of tone often results. Consider, for example, the way in which Stumpy's comic need to emphasize his alertness and mastery to offset his sense of disability ("Old cripples ain't wanted") precipitates Dude's breakdown when Stumpy shoots, as ordered, the moment someone fails to give the word on entering the jail (Dude, bathed and shaved, is unrecognizable). Everything in the film can be referred back to this unifying motif, yet, as always, it is nowhere given explicit statement. The density of the thematic development is increased by the element of parody introduced through the villains. Nathan Burdett (John Russell) goes to such lengths to get his brother out of jail not from motives of affection but from pride in his position: his actions are dictated, that is to say, by the desire not to lose face, a caricature of the motives for which the heroes act, rendered further invalid by the fact that he is defending a morally indefensible action. When Nathan tells Dude that everyone should have a taste of power before he dies, we are made strongly aware of the distinction between the kind of power Dude is experiencing in overcoming his tendency to disintegration, and the sort of power Burdett experiences.

By shifting the emphasis from man's responsibility to society (still there as a starting-point but no more than that) to his responsibility to himself, Hawks strips everything down to a basic stoic principle. From this follows his conception of friendship as a relationship based on mutual respect and mutual independence. Throughout the film we see Chance training Dude for the independence and self-respect that constitutes true manhood—for a relationship based on a balance of equality between free men. There are those who can see no more to this theme of close friendship between men in Hawks's films than the endorsement of a hearty, superficial matiness: nothing could be further from the truth. These relationships in Hawks almost invariably embody something strong, positive, and fruitful.

Here, too, the essential things are conveyed through—or more accurately perhaps *grow out of*—physical actions. It is worth quoting Hawks here—a passage from an interview he gave Peter Bogdanovich which throws much light on his methods:

> . . . we have to feel our way as we go along and we can add to a character or get a piece of business between two people and start some relationship going and then further it. In *Rio Bravo* Dean Martin had a bit in which he was required to roll a cigarette. His fingers weren't equal to it and Wayne kept passing him cigarettes. All of a sudden you realize that they are awfully good friends or he wouldn't be doing it. That grew out of Martin's asking me one day, "Well, if my fingers are shaky, how can I roll this thing?" So Wayne said, "Here, I'll hand you one," and suddenly we had something going. . . .

One moment in *Rio Bravo*, in itself very small, beautifully defines the relationship between Chance and Dude. Chance takes Dude out to patrol the streets, mainly to help him overcome the strain he is under from his need for alcohol, pauses by the paid gunman who has been appointed by Burdett to watch the jail, says "Good evening" to him and stands there till the man shuffles uneasily and moves away. We see Dude watching from the other side of the street, and from his face the impact on him of this expression of moral force, the authority that comes from integrity.

But for Hawks there comes a point where these friendships, valuable and creative as they are, reach the limit of their power to influence and affect, beyond which point the individual is alone with his own resources or sheer chance to fall back on. In *Rio Bravo* Dude's salvation rests ultimately, not on Chance, but on chance. At the climax of his relapse, when he has failed in his responsibilities and decided to hand in his badge, he clumsily pours out a glass of whiskey, nerves gone, hands trembling helplessly: it is his moment of defeat, from which it seems likely that he will never recover. Chance's example, combined with his stoic refusal to indulge him, no longer reaches him. Then, as he raises the glass, the "Alamo" music starts up again from the saloon across the street, and we see its immediate implications ("No quarter!"—it is being played on Burdett's orders) and its heroic associations strike him. He pauses, then pours the whisky back into the thin-necked bottle—"Didn't spill a drop." It is his moment of victory, and one of the great moments of the cinema. Its power to move derives partly from its context (it is, after all, one of the central moments in a film single-mindedly concerned with self-respect), partly from the irony (the tune played to undermine courage in fact has the opposite effect), and partly on our sense of the precariousness of everything.

One of the concerns common to *Red River* and *Rio Bravo* —though it takes very different forms in the two films—is a preoccupation with heroism, the conditions necessary to it, and the human limitations that accompany those conditions. This will be obvious enough in the earlier film, with its examination of the limits of the acceptability of Dunson's ruthlessness. The concept of the hero in *Rio Bravo*—of Hawks's attitude to him—may at first sight appear less complex, in that Chance is presented throughout as morally infallible. Yet Hawks's conception here is subtler. Without qualifying our sense of moral infallibility, Hawks defines in the course of the action the limitations that not only accompany it but are to some extent the conditions for its existence. Consider, for example, the song sequence, one of the film's focal points (it is often regarded as an irrelevance, forced into the action to give Ricky Nelson something to sing). It occurs just after Dude's triumph over his weakness, which in its turn was preceded by Colorado's intervention, his ceasing to "mind his own business," in the flower-pot scene. Earlier, his refusal to commit himself helped to make possible the murder of his boss, Pat Wheeler: Colorado, like Dude, was guilty of a failure of responsibility. In the song sequence he, Dude, and Stumpy sit in a circle in the jail, Stumpy accompanying on the harmonica while the other two sing. It is perhaps the best expression in Hawks's work of the spontaneous-intuitive sympathy which he makes so important as the basis of human relations. The compositions and the editing (by making us aware of the exchange of glances) as well as the acting contribute gradually to link the three men in a bond of fellow-feeling through the shared experience of the music. Throughout it, Chance stands outside the circle looking on, a paternally approving smile on his face, but none the less excluded from the common experience. The three physically or morally fallible men—cripple, reformed drunk, boy who failed once in his responsibility—are able to achieve a communion which the infallible man is denied, excluded by his very infallibility.

More obviously, Chance's limitations are revealed in his relationship with Feathers. Feathers's first appearance constitutes a humorous inversion of the fugue theme—Chance, the seemingly invulnerable, almost mythic figure of the "strong, silent man," finding his dignity abruptly undermined when the scarlet bloomers ordered for Carlos's wife are held up against him for Carlos's approval, and the woman greets him with, "Those things have great possibilities, Sheriff, but not on you." She has to take the initiative throughout their relationship; but its development is repeatedly given impetus by her attempts to drive him to establish authority over her, thereby completing his mastery of his world. Feathers, in fact, trains Chance rather as Chance trains Dude—trains him for a relationship of spiritual equals, for it is always clear that the establishment of male authority will be a matter of voluntary surrender on her part. It is true that Hawks never shows his man-woman relationships developing much beyond a certain point; nevertheless, the relationship reached at the end of *Rio Bravo* carries a beautiful and satisfying sense of maturity, with both partners strong enough to preserve a certain independence and to come together on terms of equality. Again, it is a relationship of free people, each existing from an established center of self-respect. The final scene between them, where Chance "tells her he loves her" by ordering her not to go down to the saloon to sing in the very revealing "entertainer's" costume which she wore before she knew him, far from seeming an anti-climax after the gun-and-dynamite showdown with Burdett and his men, is the true climax of the film. The lightly humorous treatment shouldn't blind us to its underlying seriousness and beauty.

There is a sense in which Chance's independence and self-sufficiency is illusory. He goes through the film systematically rejecting the help of others; yet every crisis without exception, from the arrest of Joe Burdett on, would end in disaster were it not for the unsolicited intervention of others. Without the cripple, the drunk, the comic Mexican, the teenage boy, a girl on hand to fling a well-timed flower-pot, the superman would be defeated before he had the chance to perform a single decisive action. Yet if the others are physically indispensable to him, it is never in doubt that Chance is spiritually indispensable to them. Remove him from the film, and you would be left largely with human wreckage; for it is abundantly clear that it is Chance, partly by direct influence, partly by example, by the very fact of his existence, who gives meaning, coherence, and integrity to the lives of those around him.

As a concrete embodiment of the Hawksian values, he is the nucleus round which the others can organize themselves, without which there would be no possibility of order.

I am aware that this account of *Rio Bravo* is open to one serious objection: anyone reading it, with its talk of fugues, of stylistic and structural rigor, of moral seriousness, will be totally unprepared for the consistently relaxed, delightful, utterly unpretentious film that *Rio Bravo* is. In fact, when it first came out, almost nobody noticed that it was in any sense a serious work of art. Furthermore, it would be a great mistake to assume that there is any split here between the relaxed tone and the serious content—that Hawks has "something to say," a "message," and has deliberately (and uncompromisingly) made it "entertaining," sugaring the moral pill, so to speak, for the masses. One can feel confident that *Rio Bravo* is precisely the film he wanted to make. The immense good humor is, in fact, essential to the moral tone and, together with the leisurely tempo, manifests an achieved serenity of mind; the relaxed mood of the film as a whole is never incompatible with the consistent tension in the relationships that shows the intensity of Hawks's involvement in his work.

The source of *Rio Bravo*'s richness is threefold: there is the sense of it as the product of a whole vital tradition, acting as a fruitful soil in which the film is rooted, nourishing it invisibly from beneath; and there is the sense of the film's working on many levels and for different sorts of spectators, the strength derived from its being the product and the representative of a popular art form, appealing to "groundlings" and intellectuals alike, and with no sense of discrepancy or conflict between these levels of appeal. But above all the richness derives from Hawks himself, from the warmth and generosity of his personality, pervading every scene of the film; from the essentially positive and creative nature of all the film's leading relationships; from the good humor and sanity that color every sequence. Everything in *Rio Bravo* ends happily; not a hero dies, the final battle becomes a kind of joyous celebration-party for Dude's regeneration. Yet always one is aware of the extreme precariousness of everything. In the background, never very far away, is the eternal darkness surrounding human existence, against which the Hawksian stoicism shines; over everything, coloring each scene, is the marvelous good-natured humor and balance of Hawks when he is at his best.

8

THE WILD BUNCH (1969)

Arthur G. Pettit

*Before his death in 1977, Arthur G. Pettit taught history at
Colorado College, Colorado Springs.*

Sam Peckinpah's "dirty Western," *The Wild Bunch*,[1] has probably elicited more comment than any Western movie of modern
times. Yet for all the critical attention lavished on the film, its most
distinctive feature has been largely ignored. After the opening
slaughter in the Texas town of San Rafael, the entire film is set in
revolutionary Mexico. It is this Mexico which serves as the vehicle
for Peckinpah's moral pronouncements on almost everything he
considers natural or unnatural: sex, sadism, violence, the law, the
military, the changing social order—especially the changing social
order. For all the chaos, filth, and bloodshed of the revolution (some
would say because of it), Peckinpah sees Mexico as an attractive
alternative to the increasingly automated and antiseptic United
States.

So does the Wild Bunch he created. In their rare moments of
thought each member of the Bunch realizes, with varying intensity,
that he has outlived his time and his profession; that he is a figure
apart, no more functional in the new century than the life he leads.
Pike Bishop (William Holden), puffy-eyed, pouch-jowled leader of
the Bunch whose face is a map of age and hard times, sees himself
as a living antique locked in a turn-of-the-century struggle against

Arthur G. Pettit, "The Polluted Garden: Sam Peckinpah's Double Vision of Mexico,"
Southwest Review 62 (Summer 1977). © 1977 by the *Southwest Review*. Reprinted by
permission of the publisher.

the new order. Repeatedly he tells the Bunch that each heist will be his last. As if to punctuate the fact that he knows his string is about played out, Pike talks with a pause after each line. The calendar is set against him. The miles between jobs are getting longer. The telegraph is putting the army on his trail within minutes after a robbery. The automobile is on the scene. The flying machine is just around the corner. The law is closing in; the end is clearly in sight. Yet even Pike has his fantasies. In a sentimental fireside chat with his sidekick Dutch Engstrom (Ernest Borgnine), set to the sad strains of the Mexican revolutionary song, "Adelita," Pike shows that he is still bucking the onset of autumn in his years and his occupation. Longing for an end to his career not through moral insight but because he is getting older and the law is pushing too hard, he tells Dutch, the troop's moral guardian and part-time realist, that he would "like to make just one more good score and then back off." Dutch's answer might serve as a graveyard marker for the Bunch. "Back off," he says, "to what?"[2]

The feeling of living on the edge of extinction lends a peculiar urgency to the Bunch's flight into Mexico, which becomes a journey back into history to a country where they are not yet complete anachronisms. After raiding the Texas railroad office of what turn out to be steel washers planted by the law, they are chased by bounty hunters across the border into revolutionary Mexico, where they lock horns with the antirevolutionary leader Mapache. From this point on the rebellion that changed the course of Mexican history quite literally controls the action, the thought, and the fate of the Bunch. As soon as they cross the border the entire mood of the film changes abruptly. Unlike the Texans, the Mexicans are depicted as having a flair for life. For one thing, they blend nicely with the environment. The landscape on either side of the Rio Grande looks the same, but the two races respond to it differently.

The South Texas town of San Rafael sits harshly on the land, populated with starched children, prune-faced temperance fanatics, corseted women, and buttoned-up businessmen. There are no frills, no flowers, no liquor during the South Texas Temperance Union's temporary takeover of the town, no music other than the doomsday beat of a washtub pounded by an apoplectic revivalist preacher and the earsplitting blast of an off-key Salvation Army trumpet. Once the Bunch cross the river, there is no lack of music, laughter, liquor, and color. Mexican women wear loose dresses designed to display their charms rather than tuck them in. Coquetry and lovemaking are unashamedly practiced in the open; Peckinpah's Mexicans are forever fondling, hugging, kissing, pinching. Music is at the heart of the mood Peckinpah is trying to convey. Closing our eyes in the theater, we can tell when the Bunch has forded the Rio Grande by the rousing "Mexican" orchestration, as ethnically identifiable as drumbeats announcing Indians. The sweet-sounding violins and softly stroked guitars tell us that we are now in what Angel (Jaime Sánchez), the Mexican member of the Bunch, calls "Méjico Lindo." And, although the "greaser"-hating Tector Gorch (Ben Johnson) unfeelingly remarks that the barren land on the Mexican side is "just more of Texas as far as I'm concerned," with "nothing lindo about it," we are likely to agree with Angel, who replies: "That's because you have only eyes and no heart."

Use of "ethnic" music as a manipulative sublanguage in the cinema is hardly peculiar to Peckinpah. What *is* peculiar to Peckinpah is the care he takes to set up two "Mexicos": the natural Mexico represented by Angel's lovely native village, tucked away high in the mountains, and the unnatural Mexico represented by the squalid town of Agua Verde, seized by the paramilitary General Mapache and turned into an armed camp. The scenes depicting revolutionary chaos and squalor in Mapache's garrisoned town are without equal in American cinema: the bullet-pocked walls peeling pieces of plaster like scabs on a ravaged body; the *soldaderas* cooking and washing in makeshift shanties jamming the crowded courtyard; the camp whores decked out in showy dresses and oversized army caps; the forcefully recruited campesinos looking baffled and unwarlike. A soldier, stripped to the waist, shaves in the street; a meat vendor hawks bloody turkeys; a woman, naked breasts slung with cartridge belts, suckles her child, the tiny fists nestled against the bullets.

The greasy and sadistic General Mapache (Emilio Fernández) is the lowest mudsill layer of the revolution, a nightmarish caricature of the bandit-general masquerading as revolutionary patriot while enriching himself at the expense of the people he rules through threats, assassinations, and bribes. Too dim-witted, and usually too drunk, to know what is going on, he is backed by a pair of white-linen advisers of the Imperial German Army who hold their Aryan noses against Mexican filth while attempting to bring Mapache and his army into the upcoming World War.[3] Strutting the streets of his captive village, puffing on a giant gold-label cigar, Mapache boasts to awestruck children of nonexistent victories, spills tequila down his medal-bedecked uniform, fondles breasts, squints drunkenly up skirts and down blouses, and demands that he be addressed as His Excellency. When Pike Bishop presents him with a captured machine gun, Mapache ignores the warnings of his German advisers to mount the new-fangled weapon on its tripod. Hugging the chunk of steel like a piece of firewood, he sprays peons and pottery, sending soldiers somersaulting over walls, setting women to counting their beads and children to shrieking with delight. And so it goes for several repeat performances: the rata-tat-tat of machine-gun fire punctuated with brief interludes of mad mariachi music.

It is understandable that Mapache must be enormously evil to counterpoint the glamour of the Bunch. But he is more than a singularly wicked man; he is the offal of the revolution, and he gathers similar scum about him. The wily Lieutenant Zamorra, who does the Mexican side of Mapache's thinking for him, is just as perverted as his chief and, being more intelligent, is more dangerous. The starched German advisers, lacking hearts, are even more sinister and cruel than the Mexicans they manipulate as puppets. The mass of *Mapachistas,* innocent of evil before Mapache got hold of them, are debased by the man's wickedness, which oozes through the entire town, to the point that they are all uniformly passionate, hopelessly impractical, and congenitally incapable of speaking softly or acting calmly. Mapache's Mexicans are forever killing one another, getting killed, watching others get killed, or celebrating killing. When Angel, as pure-minded as his name implies, vengefully shoots his former sweetheart Teresa, who left her native village to become a *Mapachista* whore, Mapache's mariachi band neatly sidesteps the dead woman and continues to play feverishly. In-camp murder is about as natural to these blood-soaked federal troops as drinking or making love, and far more common than meeting the enemy. The *Mapachistas* never engage the *Villistas,* but they revel in uncalled-for celebrations: showering themselves with confetti, setting off skyrockets, shampooing each other with tequila, dousing a whore's thighs with liquor and lapping it up as far as the R-rating will allow. Indeed, these Mexicans are so promiscuous and besotted that even the scrubby Gorch brothers are hard put to compete. When Mapache trots out three overworked whores to service the two brothers, the

five set out on a binge that rivals the *Mapachistas* themselves—shooting holes in wine kegs to take a drink, standing under
the spouts for a shower, stripping and bathing in a wine vat to the
tune of raucous mariachi music.

Yet for all the similarities in drinking, whoring, and killing
between the *Mapachistas* and the Bunch, Pike Bishop reminds us
three times that men under his command stick to discipline, carry
their weight, and never betray their comrades. Mapache and his
cohorts do none of those things. When not shooting off skyrockets
they are shooting off at the mouth, using surface courtesy as a mask
for deception. When the tight-lipped Bunch pride themselves on
keeping their word, Mapache promises loyalty and "fresh gorls,"
then sends a detachment of troops under a weasel-faced subordi-
nate named Herrera to kill the Bunch, who have honorably upheld
their side of the bargain to deliver guns and ammunition captured
from a U.S. Army train. Herrera, insisting that he brings love and
affection from his generals, points to the *Mapachista* troops that
line the horizon and declares: "We are friends—*all* of us." Pike,
lighting a fuse and threatening to blow up the shipment, along with
the Bunch and Herrera, cuts the odds from six Americans and
several hundred Mexicans to a personal face-down between himself
and Herrera. Screwing his dark, toothy face into the comical
grimace of a cakewalk darky, Herrera whines, "Ple-ee-ze, cot de
foose." Pike cuts the fuse and the perspiring Herrera retreats in
disgrace, showing once again that Mexican cowardice and treach-
ery are no match for the straight-talking, fast-acting Bunch.

Actually the difference between the Bunch and the *Mapachistras*
is less a matter of racial superiority and inferiority than of
ideological affiliation and environmental circumstance. When
Peckinpah turns from Mapache's brawling camp to Angel's serene
native village, we find that not all Mexicans behave like Mapache
or his brainwashed followers. In contrast to Mapache's scabby
treeless town staked out in the middle of the dun-colored desert,
Angel's cozy all-white village sits softly on the land, hugging a
slight rise of ground, seeming to sprout from Mother Earth herself.
It is surrounded by ancient shade trees, lush meadows, and a
stream. Children play at the water's edge. Plants and flowers adorn
the patios and plaza, contrasting starkly with the barren country-
side the Bunch has ridden through to get to the village. Small
groups of *pijama*-clad campesinos sit in the cool mountain sun that
holds none of the desert's bite, whiling away the after-work hours

quietly drinking pulque. Women pat tortillas, carry ollas on their heads, and promenade in the plaza, walking with barefoot grace, their loosely flowing skirts offering a pleasant contrast to the splashy tight dresses worn by Mapache's whores. There is no earsplitting mariachi music, no drunken debauchery. Old Man Sykes (Edmond O'Brien), the pioneer member of the Bunch, digs out his harmonica for the first time in years, and even the Gorch brothers behave themselves for once, helping a lovely señorita draw water from a well rather than raping her. Pike, looking on, tells the village seer that he finds the Gorches' behavior hard to believe. "Not so hard," the elder replies. "We all dream of being children again—even the worst of us—perhaps the worst most of all."

The brief interlude at Angel's peaceful village brings out the best in the Bunch. The mass slaughter at Mapache's armed town brings out the worst. When Angel is captured for smuggling guns to the *Villistas* and is dragged through the streets of Agua Verde behind Mapache's fire-engine red automobile (gift of the German Empire), his mangled body showered with skyrockets and straddled with shrieking children, the Bunch feel sorry for him but decide there is nothing they can do. Accepting a pimp's offer of whores in lieu of what is left of Angel, Pike then undergoes a dramatic conversion that makes sense only in light of a scene excised, regrettably, from the released version of the film. In a flashback to the old days, when he rode unburdened by age and a leg wound, Pike is trapped by the law in a bordello where he is wooing a married Mexican woman. Shot by the woman's husband, he flees the law and abandons the woman, who is killed by her husband. The leg wound cripples him for the rest of his career; memory of the woman haunts him in the quiet moments with a whore in Mapache's village who resembles the murdered woman. The lovely motions of the Madonna-like prostitute as she cleans herself after intercourse, accompanied by the soft strains of a guitar and the sight of a child tucked in a corner of the whore crib, evoke unfamiliar feelings of guilt, remorse, and disgust. Viewed through the delicate web of the excised flashback, Pike's decision to "go" for Angel is prompted by the nagging memory of the other woman, and by the reminder of a wasted life. Parting the blanket separating his crib from the one where the Gorch brothers are whoring together as usual, Pike says, "Let's go." The Gorches don't have to ask where. There is, quite literally, nowhere to go. The pursuing bounty hunters are waiting outside town; Mapache has them trapped inside if he wishes to dispose of them. In deciding to take revenge for Angel's torture the Bunch realize they are doomed. They also realize, however vaguely, that they are taking revenge upon themselves for having been less than human for too long.

The death march, as the Bunch wend their way through the dimly focused men, women, and children they are about to kill, is held an audaciously long time, its depth of field ensuring a gradual buildup of foreboding that conveys the poor nihilistic undertones of the suicidal commitment. What is disturbing about the commitment is that in addition to the offal of the revolution, the Bunch take so many innocent victims along with them. It is fitting that they, the Bunch, should die in a manner most closely fitted to the way they lived; less satisfying, perhaps, that there can be no distinction made between those *Mapachistas* deserving, and those less deserving, to die. When Peckinpah urges us, through the death march and the slaughter itself, to accept the dictum that dignified death may spell victory over the wasted past, we know he's talking about the Bunch. We deplore their close-up deaths because we know them well, and we applaud the close-up deaths of the bad Mexicans because we know all we care to know about them. We don't know enough about the other Mexicans to feel much of anything. The masses of *Mapachistas* who fall by bullets, grenades, and dynamite are filmed in long-distance, slow-motion shots—silhouetted against the blue sky, toppling in graceful arcs with hallucinatory grace, bouncing as from trampolines when they strike the ground. For all the kinetic beauty of cascading corpses, the bodies seem just what they are—dummies. We cannot identify with them as we can with Lyle Gorch (Warren Oates), pumping the machine gun in a fit of orgasmic release; or with Dutch, using a whore as a shield; or with Pike, shot in the back by another whore and again in the back by a venomously smiling child costumed in full military regalia. We do not think much about the villagers who suffer far more at the hands of the Bunch than they did at the hands of Mapache. We identify instead with the Bunch; their deaths are both suicide and salvation.

The wake of destruction left by the Bunch is a highly fitting end to the film. The sight of orphaned children, crippled men, and widowed women streaming out of the corpse-littered village into silent exile brings the film full circle, back to the opening massacre in the Texas town of San Rafael. It is also fitting that Old Man

Sykes, the first, last, and toughest of the Bunch, should be the sole survivor—the link to bygone days of glory when Sykes and Pike rode free of the law and unburdened by marginal members like the Gorch brothers. It is fitting too that Sykes should join the *Villistas* to put down the *Mapachistas*. There is perverse justice at work here. For all Pike's earlier doomsday lectures about the passing of the old order, and vague sense of flight into Mexico as a retreat into the past, he goes to his death through inability to accommodate his sense of revenge and remorse to practical conditions. Not so Old Man Sykes, who joins the *Villistas* through a clear sense of what it takes to survive and a vague sense of the moral goals held by their side of the revolution. The *Villistas* themselves, the white-clad *puro Indios* who rise out of the bowels of the earth to offset the glittering toy-soldier atmosphere of Mapache's khakied troops, are Peckinpah's pure-minded men of the revolution—the guardian angels of Mexico dedicated to ridding the country of the Mapaches who have raped and gutted their *patria chica* for centuries.

If the shadowy Villistas are the film's moral backdrop, Angel is the pivotal figure who innocently sets up both the physical destruction and the moral resurrection of the Bunch. It is Angel who wins our sympathy early in the film by flinging the Gorch brothers' racism in their faces; Angel who shows the Bunch an alternative to *Mapachismo* by taking them to his native village; Angel who gives the *Villistas* a case of ammunition, thus throwing Mapache into a fit of rage that leads indirectly to the deaths of Angel, Mapache, the Bunch, and most of the *Mapachistas*. By awakening the Bunch to the moral dimensions of the revolution, Angel serves as the spiritual center, the conscience and the moral burden of the Bunch. His commitment to "my people, my village, Méjico" separates him from the Bunch, who are committed only to each other until Angel's plight takes them to their deaths—if not for Angel's values, at least for his spirit. It is this moral grip held over the Bunch by Angel and what he stands for that returns to haunt us at the end of the film. As the last shot of Mapache's graveyard village, guarded by sentinel vultures, fades off the screen and we prepare to leave the theater, Peckinpah brings us back to an earlier and happier part of the story. Resurrecting the Bunch, he places us in a theater within a theater—superimposing in the center of the dark screen a small, home-movie type shot of the outlaws riding out of Angel's Elysian village earlier in the film.

As the Bunch move slowly down the flower-strewn lane beneath giant shade trees, their backs dappled by the sunlight filtering through the leaves, the entire village turns out to bid farewell, singing "La Golondrina," a song about peace and love. They doff hats, wave mantillas, toss flowers, shed tears. A comely girl hands Lyle Gorch a sombrero. The homely Dutch receives a flower. Angel bows low in the saddle to receive his mother's blessing. Pike, in a rare moment of grace, takes off his hat to the village seer. Depending on personal taste, the teary sendoff is either unbearably sentimental (the Bunch, after all, having done nothing to help the village against Mapache and having no intention of doing so) or profoundly moving.

There can be no question about where the scene fits in Peckinpah's scheme of things.[4] By following the bloody end of the film with a final nod to the Bunch in an unsullied moment of glory, Peckinpah restores any pity we may have lost for them through the slaughter. He also puts the finishing touch on his own double vision of Mexico; Mapache's Mexico and Angel's Mexico; the one of madcap music, drunkenness, filth, "dirty" sex, and violence; the other of soft music, sobriety, cleanliness, open affections, and peace. To accuse Peckinpah of separating good *Villistas* too sharply from bad *Mapachistas,* good village Mexicans from bad town Mexicans, is to catch only half the point. The entire film is played out against the backdrop of civil war, in which some of Mapache's reluctant revolutionaries were recruited from villages similar to Angel's. Yet they have become so corrupted by contact with Mapache that they, like their general, have betrayed the revolution and must pay the price. The Bunch believe they are avenging Angel by killing some Mexicans; Peckinpah believes he is ridding Mexico of a blot on the "pure" fabric of the revolution. In doing so he offers Angel's *Méjico Lindo* as an attractive alternative to Mapache's Malicious Mexico.

He also offers Angel's *Méjico Lindo* as an attractive alternative to the United States. In a recent interview Peckinpah made it clear that his interest in Mexico extends far beyond the cinema to take in a personal, social, and cultural option:

My second wife was Mexican. . . . Everything important in my life has been linked to Mexico in one way or another. The country has a special effect on me. . . . In Mexico it's all out front—the color, the life, the warmth. If a Mexican likes you, he'll touch you. It's direct. It's real. . . . Here in this country, everybody is worried about stopping the war and saving the forests and all that, but these same crusaders go out the door in the morning forgetting to kiss their wives and water the flowers. In Mexico they don't worry so goddamned much about saving the human race or about the wheeling and dealing that's poisoning us. In Mexico they don't forget to kiss each other and water the flowers.[5]

For Peckinpah, Americans are far too anxious to keep themselves clean by sterilizing themselves; far too quick to deny death by ignoring it; far too eager to strip love of meaning by romanticizing it. Angel's Mexicans, safe from the likes of Mapache, accept love and death, war and peace, as equal parts of the human tradition. They are better off for it, better able to enjoy life. Unlike the sombreroed Mexican sleepers of most American films—indeed, unlike the Bunch themselves who are quite idle when not robbing or killing—Peckinpah's Mexicans are forever *doing* things that give them pleasure: patting tortillas, picking flowers, hanging out the wash, cooking, playing, plowing, planting. More than any director to date, Peckinpah stresses Mexican ceremony and ritual—the changing work of the seasons, the richly evocative music, the villagers' graceful entertaining of the Bunch, the emotional love-making.

For all the limitations of his point of view, and for all the restrictions imposed upon him by the Hollywood action genre demanding easily identified villains and victims, Peckinpah still manages to make an important moral point: there were Mapaches aplenty in the revolution, but they had no monopoly on it. The dilemma of Mapache's Mexico is that it is already in enemy hands—not the *Villistas'* but the *Mapachistas'*—and is therefore symptomatic of all that is evil about the revolution. What the *Mapachistas* stood for, and what they wrought, was the great tragedy of the Mexican revolution. What the *Villistas* stood for, and what they eventually accomplished, is for Peckinpah the great achievement of the revolution. For all the oversimplification of the idea, by and large he is right. His way of showing us he is right is to set up two Mexicos in conflict, two warring types of Mexicans. When in the clutches of a Mapache, Peckinpah's Mexicans are physically degenerate, mentally childish, and morally bankrupt. Freed of the leeching Mapaches, they are a people of courage and compassion, dignity and grace. They can and do fight; but they don't forget to kiss each other and water the flowers.

NOTES

1. Warner Bros. Seven Arts Production, 1969; Phil Feldman, producer; Sam Peckinpah, director; screenplay by Walon Green and Sam Peckinpah, from a story by Walon Green and Roy N. Sickner; Lucien Ballard, photography; Louis Lombardo, editor; Edward Garrere, art director; Jerry Fielding, music; General de Borda (Mexican Army) and Procupio Ortiz R., advisors.

2. Arthur G. Pettit, "Nightmare and Nostalgia: The Cinema West of Sam Peckinpah," *Western Humanities Review* 29 (Spring 1975):105–22.

3. In 1915, two years after the date Peckinpah set for *The Wild Bunch*, the German emperor sent a telegram to President Venustiano Carranza of Mexico, offering to return to Mexico all territory seized by the United States in the Mexican War of 1846–48 in exchange for Mexican participation in World War I on the side of the Central Powers. The telegram was intercepted by the U.S., and Mexico, partly through fear of U.S. retaliation, partly through mixed sympathies, remained neutral.

4. Pickinpah said: "The exit from the village in *The Wild Bunch* was not in the script. I shot that in less than a day, and it's one of the high points of the picture. All of a sudden we knew the picture needed it." *Film Quarterly*, Fall 1969, pp. 8–9.

5. *Playboy*, August 1972, p. 192. In "Pat Garrett and Billy the Kid," *Sight and Sound* 42 (Spring 1973):68–69, Jan Aghed says she interviewed Peckinpah while he was in bed reading a book about Pancho Villa. Peckinpah had "a huge sheath-knife" beside him, which he later tossed into the wall. Referring to his "largely Mexico-bred semi-cult of *machismo,*" Aghed writes that Peckinpah "talked about his deep disgust with present American civilization in general and with living in California in particular. He would like to settle down in Mexico."

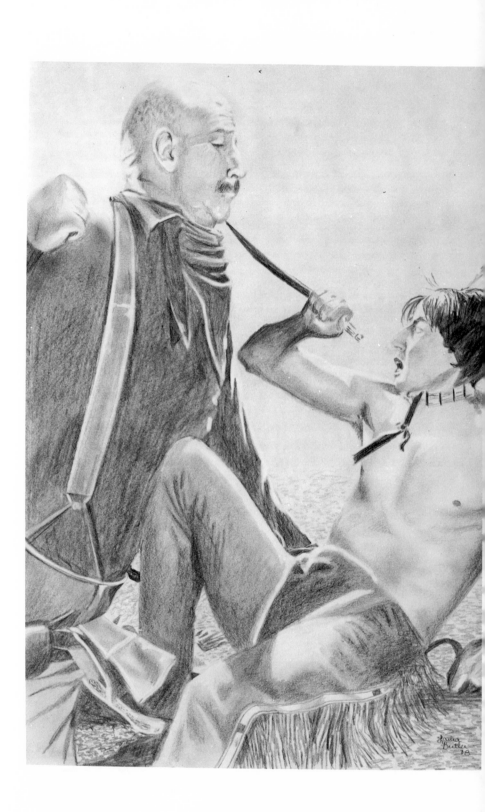

9

LITTLE BIG MAN (1970)

John W. Turner

John W. Turner teaches at Emory University, Atlanta, Georgia.

The chief difficulty with comparative studies of novels and films remains the disparity between the two media. Unless the comparison is made in terms of content or generic conventions, a critic can hardly avoid the problems involved in considering a verbal as against a visual medium. These problems are generally compounded when the discussion involves a comparison of a film made from a novel. As George Bluestone has pointed out (in *Novels Into Film*[1]), such studies usually devolve into invidious comparisons, based on unfounded assumptions about the relationship between a film and its source. The film maker, according to Bluestone, does not attempt to reproduce the novel—at least not its discursive impact—but views the novel as raw material to be transformed into presentational art.

Thus Bluestone provides a useful corrective to certain misguided attempts at comparison. But his conclusion that "cinematic and literary forms resist conversion"[2] tends to obscure the possibilities for comparative work at a new level of conceptualization, distinct from comparison *per se*, but dependent on the insights that such studies generate. In an effort to pursue these possibilities, I have attempted an analysis of Arthur Penn's film version of Thomas Berger's novel *Little Big Man*. What I have to say about the film

John W. Turner, *"Little Big Man*, the Novel and the Film: A Study of Narrative Structure," *Literature/Film Quarterly* 5 (Spring 1977). © 1977 by *Literature/Film Quarterly*. Reprinted by permission of the publisher.

speaks for itself; but I would like here to outline the principles implicit in my study.

If we are to make effective use of comparative studies of films and novels, we must first discover the appropriate grounds for comparison. The history of film suggests where the difficulty lies. In searching for an aesthetic model on which to fashion a new narrative form, early film makers (Méliès, for example) borrowed first from stage conventions and later from novelistic ones (remembering D. W. Griffith's remark on the importance of Dickens for film). The implications of Griffith's discoveries in film were articulated in the film theories of Eisenstein and Pudovkin, who explained that "the raw material of the cinema is the filmstrip itself, which is subject to no laws but those inherent in its own unique nature and form."[3] From that moment on, any attempts to compare novels and films, based on the simplified notion that either form derives narrative models directly from reality, were vitiated.

The question remains, however, what do novels and films share. The answer, simply enough, is narrative: both novels and films tell stories. What Griffith, Eisenstein, and Pudovkin were asking was how can film effectively tell a story. From this it would seem to follow that the way to approach comparisons of novels and films is through analysis of narrative. Robert Scholes and Robert Kellogg, in fact, provide the impetus for such an approach in their attempts in *The Nature of Narrative* to "break down many of the chronological, linguistic, and narrowly conceived generic categories frequently employed in the discussion of narrative."[4] It requires only an additional step to include film narrative within that same critical re-evaluation.

One problem, however, remains: the linguistic sign and the cinematic sign differ considerably. As Saussurian linguistics has informed us, language has a double articulation: that is, that a linguistic sign unites a concept (that is, a mental image) with an acoustic image (the sound of a word), and that this linguistic sign derives its meanings from within the language system. In contrast, the cinematic sign is a mechanically reproduced image of reality; the cinematic sign, therefore, refers outside its own system.

While this difference between linguistic and cinematic signs might seem to confirm the notion that film merely reproduces reality while fiction recreates it, Kuleshov's experiments with cinematic narration and geographic space demonstrate that the cinematic sign acquires additional meaning from the context in which it appears. Montage perception depends not on the individual shots, but on their sequential relationship. Meaning in film, therefore, depends on sequence, even if the viewer exercises less control over meaning than the reader of a novel.

A novel and a film, then, both tell stories; they simply tell them somewhat differently. Thus we must refrain from comparing the paraphraseable content of each version and concentrate on the act of telling. What this suggests is that novels and films can be compared on the basis of their narrative structure, on *how* they tell a story and not on *what* they tell. Thus, while film lacks the linguistic sophistication to compete with the discursive elements of fiction, it can compete successfully with the novel in terms of complex narrative structures. Orson Welles's *Citizen Kane,* to cite only a familiar example, might be considered a film that utilizes the technique of framing narratives in as sophisticated a manner as Conrad does in *Heart of Darkness.*

To effect such comparisons, one might usefully employ the recent contributions of structuralism to literary criticism. Ignoring the ideological components of structuralism, one can borrow the rudiments of structuralist methodologies—particularly the idea of binary opposition—to compare the principles of narrative structure in similar works of film and fiction. In analyzing the structure of Arthur Penn's *Little Big Man,* therefore, I have attempted to apply the idea of binary opposition to the question of translation from a literary text to a film. In the process, I have drawn parallels between the movie and the novel; but I have attempted to maintain a primary focus on the narrative structure of Penn's movie.

If Arthur Penn's *Little Big Man* has an identifiable flaw, it resides in the narrative structure of the film. Leo Braudy, in perhaps the most trenchant analysis to date, argues that the problems with the movie are a result of the inadequacies of Jack Crabb as a center of consciousness. To support this assertion, with its Jamesian overtones, Braudy contrasts the film with its source, a novel by Thomas Berger. In the novel, Braudy argues, the narrative voice of Jack Crabb is sufficient to suggest an *"aura of unity"* (my emphasis), but that when events are objectified on the screen they become disassociated from any narrative voice.[5] Thus, while Braudy recognizes Penn's attempt to retain Jack as narrator by using the voice-over of the 121-year-old Crabb on the soundtrack, he concludes that the device fails and that the movie devolves into a series of unconnected vignettes.

The problem of narrative unity that Braudy isolates here is crucial to an evaluation of the movie's structure. But before accepting his interpretation, we need to examine more closely his comments about both the novel and the film. First, the structure of Berger's novel must be more complex than Braudy indicates, since the "aura of unity" achieved by a narrative voice is not in itself a sufficient structural principle. Similarly, with the film, it is not the voice-over technique *per se* that fails, but its relationship to the order of narrative events and to the interplay of visual images. Thus a more extended comparison of the novel and the film is needed before we accept Braudy's thesis.

Thomas Berger's *Little Big Man* is the story of Jack Crabb, a man who sees himself split between loyalties to both the Indian and the white world. In the course of Jack's narrative, he travels back and forth between these two worlds. Structurally, his repeated oscillations between savagery and civilization become associated with competing definitions of the self. The fundamental contrast between savagery and civilization in the novel involves differing concepts of time. The Indian measures time in terms of the cycle of nature and believes that change is as much an appearance as a reality. White men, in contrast, believe in the linear configuration of history, where time and change are of the essence. Berger's repeated use of these contrasting notions of time warrants an interpretation of savagery and civilization as metaphors for different concepts of the self. The Indian, or circular, self involves a transcendent awareness of one's place in a timeless world; the civilized, or linear, self entails a more immediate view of one's place in a time-bound world.

When viewed as controlling metaphors in the novel, savagery and civilization define the binary opposition of the novel's structure. As *picaro*, Jack continually shifts his allegiances in the course of his adventures:

> What I had in mind on leaving the Pendrakes [he says] was of course returning to the Cheyenne. God knows I thought enough about it and kept telling myself I was basically an Indian, just as when among Indians I kept seeing how I was really white to the core.[6]

This pattern of shifting allegiances not only defines the deep structure of the novel, but provides the key to our understanding of the novel's theme of identity. What the pattern suggests is that both civilization and savagery (in the metaphoric sense) are insufficient when held in isolation. Neither the circular-spiritual self nor the linear-social self operates independently; rather, they exist as the polar opposites by which we define the continuum of identity. This polarity explains why Jack thinks like an Indian among whites and vice versa: he requires a balance of the historical and spiritual versions of the self.

Such an extended look at the structure of Berger's novel is not irrelevant to a discussion of the film by Arthur Penn. In fact, since several reviewers have argued that Penn's central concern in the movie is the problem of identity, it seems to me essential that we understand Berger's handling of that theme and the structure that embodies it. My purpose is not to establish the novel as the standard by which to judge the film, but to present an accurate appraisal of the raw materials Penn had at his disposal in order to understand the structural difficulties involved in re-creating Berger's first-person narrative on the screen.

Fundamentally, the narrative problem that Penn faced in transferring the identity theme of the novel to the medium of film was to find a cinematic equivalent for Berger's linear and circular metaphors, because it is these tropes, and not as Braudy argues Jack's narrative voice, that define the structural principle beneath Jack's oscillations between the two worlds. That this is a specifically cinematic problem can be seen from the fact that Penn attempts to include Berger's metaphors at several points in the dialogue, but that he can find no visual equivalent to reinforce their meanings. More simply, the problem is how to create credible Indians and a tangible Indian world, so as to validate cinematically the idea that Jack defines both poles of the conflict between savagery and civilization.

Penn's decision to use Indian actors to play the roles of the Cheyenne points to a commitment in this direction. But at several points in the film, Penn's comic sense deserts him and he undermines much of the credibility that he strives to create. One example of this loss of control is the character of Little Horse, a *heemaneh.* In the voice-over narration Jack explains the role of the *heemaneh* in Indian culture: "If a Cheyenne don't believe he can stand a man's life, he ain't forced to." While Jack's comment is faithful to the novel, Penn's visualization of Little Horse is not, since he relies on movie stereotypes of the homosexual. By presenting Little Horse as an "interior decorator" in Indian clothing, the movie collapses Berger's satiric contrast between Indian and white American attitudes toward sexual roles. Certainly, Little Horse is only a minor character in both the novel and the film; but this disjunction between what is said about the Indians and what we see of them is emblematic of a tendency to collapse the complex contrasts between savagery and civilization established in the novel. More than just a simplification of the novel, what we have here is a conflict in the film between its visual and auditory components, a contradiction between what it *says* and what it *is*.

While Jack's voice-over narration continually insists that we "know the Indian for what he was," the limitations of the camera make it difficult to do so. In Jack's first stay with the Cheyenne, for example, Penn tries to represent Jack's education as an Indian. In quick succession, we see Jack shooting a bow and arrow, stalking buffalo, and learning how to follow a trail. These skills, however, are only the outward manifestations of Indian life; moreover, they constitute little more than the stereotypical image of the Indian in the conventional Hollywood film. Thus they fail to communicate to the viewer what it means to do these things. The problem here, ultimately, is that what differentiates the two cultures is not what they do, but what they believe. And belief can only be limitedly represented in visual terms. As Jacks says in the novel, Old Lodge Skins "taught me everything I learned as a boy *that wasn't physical* like riding or shooting. The way he done this was by means of stories" (p. 73, my emphasis). Whereas the movie can show us Jack's physical education, his psychological growth is significantly attenuated.

The difficulties of representing Indian beliefs on the screen are most apparent with respect to the Indians' faith in spiritual powers and mysteries. In the first four chapters of the novel Berger takes great pains to validate the miraculous. As with much of the novel, these mysterious incidents progress from the comic to the more serious. In the first case, Jack proves his "manly indifference to pain" by pulling his "arrow-out-of-arse trick." The hoax is very funny, but Jack points to its larger significance: "Maybe you are beginning to understand, when I pulled the arrow-out-of-arse trick, why it didn't occur to none of the children that I was hoaxing them.

That is because Indians did not go around expecting to be swindled, whereas they was always ready for a miracle" (p. 66). Here, Jack refers indirectly to the disparity between the reader's disbelief and Indians' absolute faith in miracles. Moreover, the comic tone provides a half-way house for the reader's acceptance of the antelope hunt in the next chapter, during which Old Lodge Skins uses his "powers" to draw a magic line that brings the antelope to their destruction. Again, Berger allows Jack to mediate between the two worlds; Jack, in fact, challenges the reader's skepticism by highlighting his own doubts throughout his telling of the story. But the conviction with which he concludes carries over to the reader: "If you don't like the aspect of the affair, then you'll have a job explaining why maybe a thousand antelope run towards ruin; and also how Old Lodge Skins could know this herd would be in this place, for no animal had showed a hair before he sat down on the prairie" (p. 71).

Short of trick photography, such dramatizations of the Indians' belief in man's "power to make things happen" are impossible in Penn's film. Again, this may seem like a minor limitation, but it serves to suggest the difficulty of maintaining the significant contrasts between savagery and civilization established in the novel. The Indian's sense of time, his belief in the harmony of man and nature, and his reliance on the supernatural are all aspects of a mentality alien to the "naturalism" of Penn's cinematic representation.

As a result, Penn's attempts to develop the theme of identity are circumscribed by the difficulty in generating the binary opposition between savagery and civilization that structures the novel. In the movie, Jack's oscillations between the Indians and the whites acquire little significance beyond the comic mobility of the *picaro*. What is missing from the movie's structure are the images sufficient to embody the complex cultural differences between savagery and civilization. Without those images, Penn cannot devise a structure that will fully express the identity theme.

To criticize Penn for failing to achieve the impossible, however, is not a legitimate approach to the movie. If I have done so, I stand self-accused. What I have attempted to show is that the methodology behind Braudy's criticisms of the movie rests on an insufficient theoretical base. Braudy has identified a problem in the movie, but he has misinterpreted its cause by drawing simplistic distinctions between the novel and film as narrative forms. One cannot simply assume that there are insurmountable problems involved in translating a first-person narrative to the screen. The inadequacy of this assumption is that it rests on a Jamesian conception of the novel (as evidenced by Braudy's description of Jack's "inadequacies as a central consciousness"). Berger's novel, however, does not work in a Jamesian fashion: Jack Crabb is not Lambert Strether, nor was he meant to be. Given the picaresque form, the novel does not center on a progressive refinement of Jack's powers of perception. Thus one is forced to question Braudy's reading of the novel, not to mention his application of that reading to the film. The problem with Penn's handling of the identity theme, therefore, is less a result of Jack's limitations as a center of consciousness than it is a product of the limited metaphoric possibilities of Penn's approach.

A second reason for qualifying Braudy's criticisms of the movie is that the identity theme does not encompass all of Penn's thematic concerns, any more than it exhausts the richness of Berger's novel. As an historical novel, *Little Big Man* dramatizes the conflict between savagery and civilization which was enacted on the American Plains and which culminated in the Battle of Little Bighorn. This story, with its epic scope, seems naturally suited for cinema, where narrative breadth is readily available. Moreover, for Arthur Penn, Berger's story of the West held particular interest because of the inherent theme of American violence. In fact, from the middle of the movie on, the historical concerns tend to displace the identity theme altogether.

Penn's handling of the history is reasonably successful, although one could quibble with his handling of a number of small details. There is, for example, no justification for changing the fact that in the novel it is the Cheyenne, and not the Pawnee (as it is in the movie), who kill Jack's family. While slight, this change could be interpreted as representative of a larger tendency to sentimentalize the Cheyenne and vilify the whites. Such a tendency runs counter to Berger's complex satire, in which both ways of life receive a mixture of blame and praise. Nevertheless, despite these simplifications, Penn reproduces the essence of the historical theme: the acculturation of the Indian. Certainly, the single most effective scene in the movie—the massacre at Washita—vividly dramatizes the violence of the historical conflict. However, the very effectiveness of the scene has raised another set of questions about the structure of the movie.

According to Pauline Kael, Penn's portrayal of the violence of the conflict violates the form of the movie. As she sees it, the comic picaresque form cannot support the arresting violence of the massacre scene:

> For the tall tale to function as an epic form, the violence must be wry and peculiar, or surreal and only half-believable—insane, as it is in the book, and not conventionally bloody like this. . . . To be successful, the picture must deepen by comic means, and when Penn goes for seriousness he collapses the form of the movie.[7]

As with the criticism of Braudy, Kael's comment points to a structural problem in the film, but it does not provide adequate explanation. Once again, we must look more closely at both the novel and the film to interpret the formal difficulties.

Whatever else can be said, Penn handles the massacre scene extraordinarily well: sight and sound are more effectively combined in this scene than anywhere else in the movie. The setting, with its muted effect of snow, provides the perfect visual counterpoint for the horror of the violence that follows. At the same time, the gently rising soundtrack of "Garry Owen" combines with visual images of a dream-like advance of the soldiers to rivet the viewer's attention. We even find ourselves caught up in the visual poetry of Penn's panorama and the martial fervor of "Garry Owen," until the beauty explodes in violence. Penn's editing at this point is most expressive: by alternating shots of increasingly shorter temporal length, Penn heightens the tension of the scene, which climaxes with the death of Jack's wife, Sunshine. Jack and Sunshine hit the ground simultaneously, causing the audience to writhe with Jack in impotent horror as the visual and auditory montage culminates in the silence of Jack's agony and the stillness of Sunshine's death.

This arresting silence at the center of the Washita massacre marks the structural fulcrum of Penn's film. Significantly, the earlier identity theme coalesces with the historical theme at this point, since Jack is transformed from a passive figure into one strongly motivated by revenge. The revenge motif in the second half of the movie, in fact, is Penn's creation, because in the novel Jack remains more acted upon than active throughout the book. The problem with the change is not that it represents a violation of the sanctity of Berger's novel—because it is potentially the solution to many of the problems of translation—or even that it subverts the comic form of the first half of the movie; rather, the problem is that

Penn does not accept the implications of the change in his thematic focus.

Given the violence of the Washita scene, and given the change in Jack's character, one expects a change in the remainder of the film. If the silence at the center of the massacre is to serve as a structural fulcrum, then the movie must turn to something new. What is at issue here, therefore, is a problem of tonal control. To prevent the violence of the massacre from collapsing the structure of the movie, the comedy of the second half must be tinged with darkness. The tonal control of the rest of the movie, however, is decidedly uneven. Unfortunately, what happens is that the movie reverts too often in the second half to the comedy of Jack's earlier picaresque adventures. As a result, the underlying conception of the film becomes confused and the narrative structure collapses. The problem, then, is not so much with the scene itself (as Kael suggests), but with what follows it.

Disorienting tonal confusions occur at two significant points in the latter half of the narrative. The first of these, when Jack is down and out, is difficult to discuss, because the problem seems to reside less in Penn's conception than in the execution of the actor, Dustin Hoffman. Structurally, the design of the down-and-out sequence is perfect. The episode follows directly after Jack's failure to effect his revenge by killing Colonel Custer. Jack's enforced recognition that "he is no Cheyenne brave" logically precipitates his despair. Yet, the despair is not maintained with any consistency.

Theoretically, the sequence should work to reinforce the structural fulcrum, since Penn contrives parallels to earlier scenes by bringing back the most important minor characters—Wild Bill Hickok, Mrs. Pendrake, and Allardyce Meriweather. But Jack's response to these visitations from the past is too reminiscent of the earlier scenes. Rather than emphasizing the difference in Jack's character after Washita (predicated in the film version), the sequence has the effect of contradicting our sense of the change. Since the potential for establishing a sense of difference is inherent in the structural parallels, one must assume that it is the limitations of Dustin Hoffman's performance that create the confusion. One could argue, at least, that Hoffman fails to communicate the bitterness that is a requisite for the success of this narrative sequence. There is too much of the charming insouciance of the *picaro* in Hoffman for him to handle the scene with Mrs. Pendrake in the brothel. The scene needs to be filled not simply with Jack's recognition of the logical development of Mrs. Pendrake's character, but also with an emotional response that brings into play what he has lived through since his earlier experiences in the world of civilization. Hoffman's wry innocence, however, fails to convince us of the change in Jack Crabb predicated by the film's structure. Rather, the effect is to temper the importance of the revenge motif, causing the Washita massacre to seem like an anomaly in the structure of an otherwise comic tale.

While the tonal confusion here seems less a product of intention than execution, the same cannot be said of the movie's ending. Once again, given the way the massacre scene fixes our attention on the violence of the historical conflict, there is no aesthetic justification for Penn's lapse into comedy. One measure of the weakness of this comic ending is manifested in the omissions from the novel. Paralleling the earlier tendency to soften the Cheyenne character, Penn avoids any direct reference to the Indian practices of mutilating the bodies of their dead enemies. Penn also avoids the most important dramatic confrontation of the novel, which is anything but comic, between Jack and Old Lodge Skins: "Well, speak of shame, there was me. I still had not commenced to explain my presence with Custer. If indeed it could be explained, I had to try." In the movie, Old Lodge Skins inexplicably accepts Jack with open arms. And Jack does not feel compelled to explain.

But the major problem with the ending consists of the comic undermining of Old Lodge Skins. In the novel, the Indian chief wills his death. In the movie, Old Lodge Skins's gesture ends with his comic re-awakening and his statement that "sometimes the magic doesn't work." One can see parallels here with the earlier problem in the movie of handling the Indians' supernaturalism. But, more importantly, the comic ending undermines the historical sense of the movie by avoiding the ironies inherent in the Battle of Little Bighorn. Although the defeat of Custer marks the height of Indian military success, historians have recognized that the battle also marks the beginning of the end of the Indian wars. William T. Hagan, in fact, ironically entitles his chapter on Little Bighorn, "The Warrior's Last Stand."[8] With the disappearance of the buffalo and with the renewed vigor of army operations after Custer's defeat, the Indian was forced to abandon the hope that the tide of civilization could be stemmed or that his old way of life could easily be maintained. In the novel, Berger captures this ironic sense of the Indian defeated even in victory by concluding Jack's narrative of the battle with the death of Old Lodge Skins:

> Though I was only thirty-four years of age, I felt in some ways older than I do now. Now it is only one man's life that is about to end; then it was a whole style of living. Old Lodge Skins had seen it all, up there on Custer Ridge, when he said there would never be another great battle. I didn't get his point immediately, and maybe you won't either, for there was many a fight afterward, and mighty fierce ones, before the hostile Plains tribes finally give up and come in permanent to the agencies. (p. 444)

More than simply the death of one man, the death of the old chief symbolizes the death of a mode of life.

Penn's comic ending, therefore, not only undermines the dignity of Old Lodge Skins, but also raises questions about Penn's historicism. To a great extent, Penn seems to resist the historical implications of the conflict on the Plains. By opting for a sentimental ending, Penn undermines the effectiveness of his cinematic achievement in the Washita scene, and leaves himself open to the criticisms of Pauline Kael. As we have seen, Kael is right about the massacre scene, but for the wrong reason. It is not that Penn should have excised his thematic seriousness; it is not even that "the film must deepen by comic means" alone, but that, having introduced a serious concern for history, Penn does not follow that theme to its tragic end as Berger does.

As a result, the movie lacks the closure that its story demands. Having entered the arena of history, Penn obligates himself to a narrative structure that rests on the opposition between the past and the present. Although Jack Crabb lives to tell his story, in the novel he knows that his story ended at Little Bighorn. In the movie, however, we miss that sense of an ending: Jack and Old Lodge Skins wander slowly back down the mountain, as if into the future. Their humorous discussion of sex furthers this sense of ongoing life. But the inconclusiveness of such an ending collapses the structure that Penn has striven to create. If Washita is to be the structural center of the movie, then it must mark the beginning of the end. What we have at the end, however, is an avoidance of closure, a relapse into comedy when it is least appropriate; the necessary somber note is totally absent.

The movie fails, then, despite all of Penn's admirable intentions and considerable craftsmanship, because he has not achieved a structure that will sustain the weight of his materials. Penn's reluctance to close off the movie's structure points to the weaknesses of his artistic conception. What vitiates Penn's achievement in the film is his failure to avoid romanticizing the past. As Leo Braudy puts it: "Penn, in fact, seems torn between preserving the past through the clarity of photographic detail and preserving the past through the romantic versions of reality that are available in myth."[9] This tension between romance and fact is nowhere more evident than in the contrast between the grim reality of Washita and the nostalgic longing of the final scene. Moreover, this conflicting attitude remains unresolved, so that the structure of the film is impaled on the horns of its own divided loyalties.

A comparison of the film and novel, therefore, is justified not because Penn either does or does not take liberties with Berger's novel, but because the comparison reveals the source of the flaws in the movie's structure. Unlike the novel, the movie fails to sustain either of the binary oppositions necessary for its structure. Understandably, Penn has minimal success establishing the savagery and civilization contrast in Berger's novel, because that opposition depends on the discursive and metaphoric aspects of language. But, less understandably, Penn also fails to maintain the separation between past and present implicit in the frame story. Without either of these oppositions to give meaning to Jack's narrative, the structure collapses.

Thus, while we cannot criticize Penn for failing to reproduce Berger's novel on the screen, we can compare the strengths and weaknesses of their respective narrative structures. Such an approach to a film version of a novel is useful because it provides the grounds for comparison without resorting to the usual criterion of fidelity to the original text. One should not expect the movie to reproduce all of the novel's complexity, or even reproduce all of its thematic concerns; but one can expect the movie to establish a viable narrative structure. And therein lies the difficulty with Penn's version of *Little Big Man*.

NOTES

1. George Bluestone, *Novels Into Film* (Berkeley: University of California Press, 1971).

2. Ibid, p. 218.

3. David A. Cook, "Cinematic Speech: A History of Models," *The Master Reel* No. 2 (March 1975):3.

4. Robert Scholes and Robert Kellogg, *The Nature of Narrative* (New York: Oxford University Press, 1966), p. 6.

5. Leo Braudy, "The Difficulties of *Little Big Man,*" *Film Quarterly* 25 (Fall 1971):30.

6. Thomas Berger, *Little Big Man* (Greenwich, Connecticut: Fawcett Publications, 1964), p. 160. Further references to *Little Big Man* are cited in the text.

7. Pauline Kael, "Epic and Crumbcruncher," *Deeper Into Movies* (Boston: Little, Brown, 1973), p. 213.

8. William T. Hagan, *American Indians* (Chicago: University of Chicago Press, 1961), pp. 113–142.

9. Braudy, "The Difficulties," p. 30.

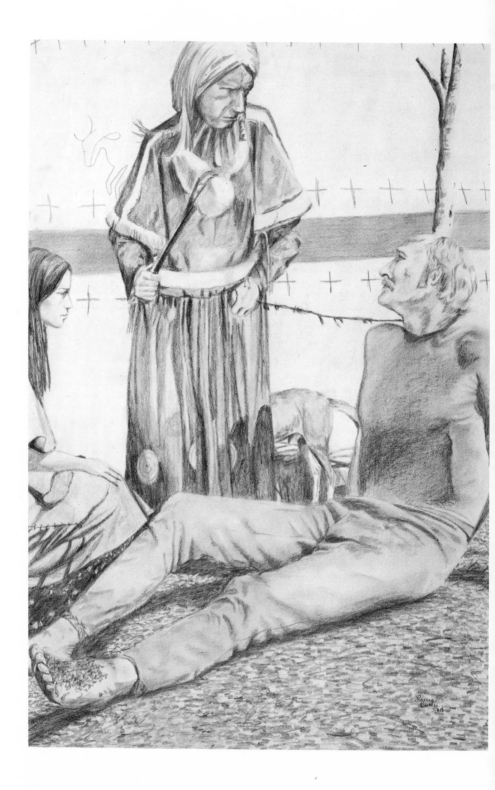

10

A MAN CALLED HORSE (1970)

Dan Georgakas

Dan Georgakas lives in New Jersey and is the author of The
Broken Hoop *and* Red Shadows, *a two-volume history of the
American Indians published in 1973.*

The American Indian has been an essential dramatic ingredient
in Hollywood's epic of the West, and a key element in the vision of
America and its destiny embodied there. Whether we take the
Indian's role as that of the abominable id—a projection of the
bestiality white culture could not face in itself—or as a stand-in for
the hostile "nature" that Americans thought they could overcome,
it is hardly surprising that with the turmoils, re-evaluations, and
rebellions of the sixties a different image of the Indian should have
begun to emerge in American films. Recent Indian films make a
point of advertising their sympathy for the Indian point of view.
Generally "real" Indians play all minor Indian roles and occasionally even major speaking parts. At first sight, no effort seems too
great to obtain an aura of authenticity in regard to speech, music,
customs, and history. Usually white guilt is admitted through the
device of at least one rabid saliva-at-the-mouth racist ready to
command a massacre of a sleeping village. This beast is contrasted
to the dignified Indian spokesman who is invariably peace-minded.
Such an approach is an improvement over the grunts and howls of
an earlier period but only at the lowest level: the new films tell us
very little about the Native Americans and even less about
ourselves and our own history.

Dan Georgakas, "They Have Not Spoken: American Indians in Film," *Film Quarterly* 25
(Spring 1972). © 1972 by *Film Quarterly*. Reprinted by permission of the publisher.

On the surface, Elliot Silverstein's *A Man Called Horse*, which uses some five hundred Sioux actors, might seem the most authentic of recent films that portray Indians. The Sioux language makes up eighty percent of the dialogue, the impressive Sun Dance ceremony is a central plot element, and all the action takes place within an Indian environment. The headdresses, dwellings, artifacts, masks, and ceremonial paint are as genuine as research can make them. The only trouble is that all this authenticity is an illusion and a waste. The film is fantasy from start to finish.

The year is 1825 and Lord Morgan (Richard Harris), an English aristocrat on a hunting expedition, is captured by a Sioux band led by Yellow Hand (Manu Tupou). The Englishman is not treated as a human being but as a horse. He is given to Yellow Hand's harridan mother, Buffalo Cow Head (Dame Judith Anderson), who ties him to a stake. This is all wrong. The Sioux had a tradition of hospitality toward strangers. Anyone so odd looking as the yellow-haired, pale-faced Wasichu (a term for Europeans that had no racial overtones) would be treated with great curiosity and respect, much as Lewis and Clark had been treated a decade earlier. Even if the encounter had turned hostile, there would not be torture and the kind of abuse shown, for that was not the Sioux way. The idea that a man should be tied up and treated as an animal is something that might have occurred to the New England Puritans, but it was as far from Sioux thinking as hunting for pleasure instead of need.

The Englishman learns the ways of the Indian slowly and Silverstein comes up with an interesting device in handling the translation. The Indians speak only Sioux and Morgan/Horse speaks only English. A captive French half-breed (a European designation, by the way) supplies minimal translations and interpretations of strange acts. This de-emphasis on dialogue makes the kind of demands on a director the silent screen once made and calls attention to the Indian trappings. One almost wishes there was no dialogue at all for almost everything the half-breed says is nonsense.

Horse's moment to impress the Sioux comes when a group of Shoshone creep up on the camp when the warriors are absent. Horse slays the intruders and is immediately elevated to human and warrior status. This dramatic turnabout would be likely, as Sioux placed importance on what individuals did and most likely would have interpreted Horse's actions as having the favor of the spirits. That Yellow Hand's daughter, Running Deer (Corrina Tsopei), falls in love with Horse is also credible as the Sioux were a romantic people and the strange white warrior who might possess special magic would be an extremely attractive figure.

But to establish full membership in the tribe, Horse undertakes the Sun Dance ceremony, and here the film is simply sacrilegious in terms of Indian beliefs. The Sun Dance was not designed to show individual courage to other men or to win a bride. The Sun Dance was the highest religious rite of the Sioux. In it, a man proved his humility and worthlessness to the spirits by mortifying his flesh. Elaborate purification rites were absolute prerequisites, as a successful dance might bring a vision of use to the entire tribe. Skewers were fastened under a man's flesh and he attempted to pull loose by dancing. The pain was caused by his own acts and the onlookers pitied him and encouraged him with song and music, praying he would have an important vision. (Sitting Bull performed the Sun Dance before Custer's attack. He lost some sixty pieces of flesh but had a vision which foretold the coming triumph.) In *Horse* the ceremony is reduced to a primitive sadistic test of courage in which the vision is a delirious by-product.

Naturally, Morgan-now-Horse is successful in the Sun Dance and marries Running Deer. He sees this as another step toward his escape. His problem is cut short by a massive Shoshone raid. Again the film falls apart historically. The men of the plains never waged war in European fashion; small bands went out to steal horses or to fight small engagements more akin to dueling than war. The highest honor was to "count coup," which was to touch a living opponent still surrounded by his fighting comrades with a ceremonial stick shaped like a shepherd's staff. Killing an enemy was a less important coup. In *Horse,* the Shoshone attack like U.S. cavalry. Horse-still-Morgan saves the day when he lines up the tribal youth in English archery rows and their arrows cut down the Shoshone who attack like the Light Brigade itself. Yellow Hand dies in the battle and tribal leadership falls to Horse. Running Deer also dies conveniently, but Horse shows his sensitivity to his new post by taking the harridan Buffalo Cow Head as his own mother. She waits for spring to die so that he can have good weather for his return to England.

Rather than a tale of Indian life, *Horse* is really about a white nobleman proving his superiority in the wilds. Almost every detail of Indian life is incorrect. An angry Sioux writing in the *Village Voice* complained about the treatment of the Sun Dance. He also noted that the Sioux never abandoned widows, orphans, and old people to starve and freeze as shown in the film. He points out that the cuckold husband in the film would not have lamented as shown but would have wiped out his disgrace by charging ten enemies single-handed. The writer adds that even something as simple as kissing on the lips is incorrect, for the custom did not come to the Sioux until mid-century. The list of such mistakes and inaccuracies is as long as the film itself.

Stripped of its pretentions, *Horse* parades the standard myth that the white man can do everything better than the Indian. Give him a little time and he will marry the best-looking girl (a princess, of course) and will end up chief of the tribe. It is also interesting that Yellow Hand and Running Deer look very European while some of the nastier Indians are darker with flat features. Sioux features in fact did range from Nordic to Mongol and their color from white to copper red, but this case seems the usual pandering to ideas of Anglo-is-beautiful.

The Sioux were called the Vision Seekers because they placed so much importance upon receiving communications from the spirits in the form of visions. They were cheerful people very fond of jokes, games, and romance. Above all, they liked to feast, dance, and sing. None of this comes through in *Horse*. Even the use of the native language becomes a handicap, for eloquence was another Sioux characteristic. Without their own words much of the beauty of their way of life is lost. The half-breed's silly interpretations should be compared to some of the speeches of the Sioux holy man Black Elk to see how much has been lost:

> You have noticed that everything an Indian does is in a circle, and that is because the Power of the World always works in circles, and everything tries to be round . . . The sky is round and I have heard that the earth is round and so are all the stars. The wind, in its greatest power, whirls. Birds make their nests in circles, for theirs is the same religion as ours.

11

THE GREAT NORTHFIELD MINNESOTA RAID (1972)

Don Graham

Philip Kaufman's *The Great Northfield Minnesota Raid*, released in 1972, is the most recent movie to be made about the life of the celebrated outlaw Jesse James. A color film, it opens, as the credits unfold, with a black-and-white documentary depicting Okie-like families being driven from worn-out farms. A narrative voice intones that fresh winds of change have begun to blow across the land, the clothing of the farmers ripples in the rhetorical winds, and the audience enjoys the first of many laughs to come. The documentary opening does more than set a comic tone, however; it alludes directly to the most famous of the Jesse James films, Henry King's *Jesse James* (1939). Originally Kaufman's prologue was longer and evoked other Jesse James movies, but the studio, Universal, insisted that this material be shortened to the single piece of documentary footage. This is too bad because it would be interesting to know which other James films Kaufman found significant; certainly he had plenty to choose from, for there have been no less than twenty-five James movies, ranging from works by important directors such as Fritz Lang (*The Return of Frank James*, 1940) to fluffs like *Jesse James Meets Frankenstein's Daughter* (1966).

Kaufman's use of King's film tells us a great deal about how to

Don Graham, "*The Great Northfield Minnesota Raid* and the Cinematic Legend of Jesse James," *Journal of Popular Film* 6 no. 1 (1977). © 1977 by *The Journal of Popular Film*. Reprinted by permission of the publisher.

understand the intentions of *The Great Northfield Minnesota Raid,*
and further, it confirms some methodological assumptions about
ways to study the allusive rhetoric of self-conscious Westerns and
the tradition of legendary cinematic heroes.[1] First of all, Kaufman
seems to have had in mind something similar to the opening of Don
Siegel's *The Shootist* (1976), which presents a concise cinematic
history of John Wayne's progress from youthful Western hero to
aging Western hero, preparing us for the dying Western hero of the
actual movie. Kaufman hoped to show, he has written me, the
"sense of Jesse James as a hero who came out of movies."[2] In such a
revisionist approach, the target becomes, again in Kaufman's
words, the "bogus history we're generally given in movies."[3] With
this context of explicit and implicit reference in mind, it is
instructive to recall King's film and its assumptions in order to
appreciate what Kaufman has done.

The history given us in King's film is a kind of Grapes-of-Wrath
Populism. Jesse (Tyrone Power) and Frank (Henry Fonda) are
honest tenant farmers subjected to abuse and exploitation by an
evil alliance of bankers and railroad monopolists, in short by the
unholy power of post-Civil War Yankee capitalism. All the villains
are city-slicker types wearing shiny Eastern-cut suits. Facts are
distorted to fit the economic theme. Jesse's mother, who in "real
life" lost a hand from a bomb thrown into the James home, loses
her life in the film. Her death becomes the central emotional
impetus for the James boys turning into outlaws. This decision and
the consequent raids upon banks and trains are supported by
Populist assumptions. The old newspaper editor acclaims Jesse and
writes fire-and-brimstone editorials denouncing lawyers, governors,
railroads, and dentists. At the same time Jesse's popularity with his
constituency, the other sodbusters, preachers, and common people
in Missouri, increases until Jesse James is a true folk hero. In the
eulogy that concludes the film, the old editor, finding words to
commemorate a monument at Jesse's grave, pronounces Jesse bold,
lawless—but with plenty of reasons—good at his trade, and, finally,
the "goldurndest buckaroo" there ever was. Nearly all the key
elements of Jesse's life are present: his agrarian background, his life
of crime, his marriage (also much idealized), his betrayal, death,
and apotheosis. The single omission is the Civil War years, when
Jesse was a raider with "Bloody" Bill Anderson's guerilla band.
This pre-criminal life of violence might have deflected our
attention away from the economic theme of Jesse's justified actions

against the railroad-banker alliance. In any case, King's decision to exclude the Civil War years indicates the utility and adaptability of the James legend. Like Arthurian lore, the James story lends itself to differing interpretations by means of omissions, refocusings, and imaginative inventions.[4]

The economic thesis of King's *Jesse James* is what now dates the film and makes it irrevocably of the 1930s. But as I have suggested, Kaufman is less interested in the substance of King's treatment than in the stylized creation of a romantic and false celluloid hero. Kaufman's film, therefore, is at one level a calculated demolition of the movie-star Jesse James. The break with King's version of the legend is sharply established in the first appearance of the outlaw leader. In King's film we first see Jesse as a young, incredibly handsome yeoman farmer. Standing in a garden, smiling, leaning on a hoe, Tyrone Power seems to be wearing a halo designed by Thomas Jefferson. In Kaufman's opening scene, after the black-and-white prologue, a plain-featured Jesse, played brilliantly by Robert Duvall, is sitting beside his brother Frank (John Pierce) on a two-hole toilet. Looking at the wiping paper (which instead of a mailorder catalogue is a Northfield bank prospectus) Jesse finds plans for a raid on the bank scribbled by a previous occupant, Cole Younger. This unglamorous, comic beginning introduces a series of devastating reversals of the romantic legend.

By the time Kaufman is finished, nothing of the movie-hero Jesse James remains. Jesse as Robin Hood? Hardly. He makes a mortgage payment for a kindly grandmother, then kills the banker who collected the money and leaves a clue beside the body to frame the old woman. And if this isn't enough, he later kills the old woman in order to effect his escape from Minnesota. Jesse as Romantic Lover? Hardly. He self-righteously and neurotically abstains from carnal pleasure at a brothel the night before the raid; and in the only reference to Jesse's wife, Cole Younger hints that, sexually, Jesse is a joke. Jesse as Civil War Hero? Here, too, the debunking is apparent. For Kaufman's Jesse the War is still on in 1876, and the bank raid is an act of guerilla warfare carried out against a sinful Northern stronghold. A crazy guerilla fighter, Jesse takes no prisoners and kills every Yankee he can, soldiers, civilians, women. Jesse as Adventure Hero? No. The escape from Minnesota in the King movie is a long dive by horseback into a river from a high cliff, the essence of spectacle, courage, and excitement. But in Kaufman's film Jesse sneaks southward in a buckboard, dressed in the garments of the grandmother whom he likes to call "Mother" and whose blood soils these very garments. He is the epitome of the unheroic, unscrupulous, and blood-thirsty villain. He is also very funny. One of Duvall's triumphs—and Kaufman's—is to turn a character frozen in the absurd rigidity of an "hysterical, psychopathic, religious maniac" into a comic figure.[5]

If King's film creates a myth, Kaufman's debunks one myth, creates another, and probes in complex ways the sources of myth-making. Kaufman's Jesse is keenly aware of his fame, of his role in enacting a high destiny. He has visions, he dotes on his reputation, and after the Northfield raid, which is a complete disaster—two of the gang are killed, several are wounded, and there's not a cent to show for the day's work—he can only think self-exultantly that this raid "will be talked about forever and ever." Jesse's larger-than-life conception of himself seems to derive from frontier protestantism. He is a kind of demonic protestant stereotype; thus he identifies himself with God's plans—mainly, wreaking havoc upon the Sodom-Gomorrah cities of the North; he is sexually frigid; and he is a coldblooded, self-absorbed killer.

Against Jesse's manic righteousness, Kaufman sets the real folk hero of the film, Cole Younger (Cliff Robertson). Cole Younger is a folk hero ironically aware of his status. He likes to spin yarns and through his personal warmth and talltales can beguile men lounging around storefronts. Cole likes to treat his own exploits ironically. On the trip north to catch up with Jesse's half of the gang, he describes the journey as a "knightly quest." The purpose of the quest is to rob the bank in order to get funds to counterbribe the Missouri state legislature which, having voted the outlaws amnesty, has now reversed itself because of a Pinkerton agent's bribe. Cole can play the political games of his day with aplomb. (Incidentally, emphasizing amnesty and corruption in government parallels the political content of King's film.)

The sources of Cole's heroic status are both ancient and modern, magical and ultra-materialistic. Cole wears a magical protective vest that is also a model of practical ingenuity. Twice in the film he survives multiple gunshot wounds, thanks to the leather corset enveloping his chest. Even when the pain is so great that, comically, his eyes cross, Cole is able to get up. This is what heroes have to do, Cole tells us; if you don't get up, you're dead. Each time is a minor resurrection, and we are forced to see that Cole can't be killed. In an early scene the primitive roots of Cole's imagination are set dramatically against Jesse's crazy Calvinism. Severely wounded, Cole is taken to a cave where an old crone, a herb doctor, stews up a mess of poultices to restore Cole's health. Her incantations of snakes and frogs' eyes and the like vibrate against Jesse's rabid exhortation to the gang. He spits out a Christian vision of the upcoming raid on Northfield as though he were speaking in tongues.

Surely the most interesting dimension of the Cole Younger figure is his profound interest in the present and the future. The present, of course, is 1876, the year of the American Centennial celebration, a time when important inventions contended with mechanical oddities for people's attention. On the train ride north, Cole looks at a mechanics magazine and is fascinated by intricate drawings of new machines. He also knows about A. G. Bell's recent invention, which is an acute perception indeed considering that at the Centennial Exhibition in Philadelphia, the telephone was mostly ignored in favor of larger, more sensational machines such as the Corliss engine. In Cole's view all inventions are "wonderments." He has a wide-eyed interest in everything from steampowered tractors to a new game called baseball. Cole is unique among Western heroes in recent films (let's say from *Ride The High Country* [1962] on) in that he can accommodate himself to the progressive present. In many Westerns some machine, not infrequently the automobile, spells the end of a way of life; in *The Ballad of Cable Hogue* (1970), for instance, an automobile runs over the hero at the end. Cole however lives on into the next century, dying in 1916. Cole, the narrative voice tells us at the movie's close, lived to "see the birth of a new age."

The new age is starkly foretold through the superb visual presentation of Northfield. I know of no town like Kaufman's in previous Western movies. Again King's film provides an instructive model. In the 1939 movie the James gang, clad in long white trail dusters (which is historically accurate), rides into a conventional Western studio town, the kind one has seen in thousands of Western movies. You can't distinguish King's Northfield from Abilene or Dodge City. In Kaufman's treatment though, Northfield is decidedly un-Western looking.[6] It's a town of shops and shop-keepers; there's even a bakery. The town looks European, or better, Scandinavian, and the Southerners feel this foreignness keenly. As they ride into Northfield, one of the gang wonders why the people are celebrating the Centennial. "Hell," he says, "they ain't even

Americans." In their long white dusters, worn to signify that they are cattle drovers and buyers, and to hide their side arms, the James and Younger boys are ghostly anachronisms from a frontier past. In 1876, Northfield had more colleges than banks, two to one respectively. Kaufman knows this and shows the Younger brothers riding past an immaculate campus with undergraduates strolling about on manicured lawns. Colleges, bakery shops, a town baseball team, steam tractors and steam calliopes—this is a town well on its way to gadgetry and babbittry. Yet it is also a town with strong ties to America's frontier vigilante tradition. Threatened by the James gang, the Northfieldians rise up in unified opposition and succeed in preventing the robbery. The aroused citizenry goes on to hang some innocent sinners discovered at a whorehouse out in the country and attempts to slaughter the remnants of the outlaws. The thing that unites the old America and the new America, the film implies, is a joyous predilection for violence, for gunplay. After all, as Cole tells a local baseball enthusiast, shooting, not baseball, is the national pastime.

It should be clear by now that Kaufman's revisionist study of bogus history as purveyed in Jesse James movies is not itself free of bogus elements. This is as it should be, for the Western movie has never purported to *be* history, only to use it and interpret it. Through a combination of mimesis and myth, history and fantasy, *The Great Northfield Minnesota Raid* both exploits and enriches the genre. Whether it has laid poor Jesse in his movie grave remains to be seen.

NOTES

1. Most reviewers looked to recent Westerns for a context in which to place Kaufman's film. Noting the violence, anti-heroism, and raunchy sex, they found echoes and analogues in such works as *The Wild Bunch, Butch Cassidy and the Sundance Kid, McCabe and Mrs. Miller, The Left-Handed Gun, Bonnie and Clyde,* and *Tell Them Willie Boy Is Here.* See, for example, Michael Dempsey, *The Great Northfield Minnesota Raid,"* Film Quarterly 25 no. 4 (Summer 1972):47–9; and Richard Schickel, "Made of Myth," *Time,* July 10, 1972, pp. 68–9.

2. Letter from Philip Kaufman to Don Graham, September 7, 1976.

3. *Ibid.*

4. Commenting on the popularity of movies about Jesse James, Leo Braudy argues that the basic appeal comes from "the split between the normal, peaceful self and the dark marauding self" represented by the outlaw hero. *The World In a Frame: What We See in Films* (Garden City: Doubleday, 1977), p. 139.

5. Philip French, *"The Great Northfield Minnesota Raid,"* *Sight and Sound* 43 (1973–74):55.

6. *Ibid.* French makes an astute comment about the town's appearance: ". . . the burgeoning post-frontier community of Northfield has a convincingly raw yet truly inhabited feel rare in Westerns."

12

ULZANA'S RAID (1972)

Jack Nachbar

*Jack Nachbar teaches English and popular culture at Bowling
Green State University, Bowling Green, Ohio. He is co-editor of
The Journal of Popular Film and Television.*

Robert Aldrich's 1972 U.S.-Cavalry-versus-the-Indians Western,
Ulzana's Raid, received some favorable response during its initial
showings, but in general the film was and is still being victimized
by the period of its release. The early 1970s was a period of ex-
ceptional creative skill and innovation in Western movies. As a result, *Ulzana's Raid* seems to pale next to some of its more flashy
contemporaries. It is less realistic than *Monte Walsh* (1970) and *The
Hired Hand* (1971). On the other hand, it is less obviously mythic
than *The Cowboys* (1972), *Jeremiah Johnson* (1972) or *High Plains
Drifter* (1973). It is less technically innovative than *McCabe and
Mrs. Miller* (1971) and *The Great Northfield Minnesota Raid* (1972).
And it does not re-examine tested Western plots as *The Culpepper
Cattle Company* (1972) reconsiders cattle-drive Westerns and *Bad
Company* (1972) explores Western outlawry. Even though it is less
experimental both thematically and technically than other early
1970s Westerns, *Ulzana's Raid* is nevertheless an important contribution to the evolution of Western films. By presenting a dialectic
rather than a one-sided perspective on the Indian-white struggles on
the closing American frontier, Aldrich's film is both a climactic
summary of the hundreds of Indian uprising films from the past and

a suggester of a new direction, as yet unfulfilled, that such pictures may take in the future.

Ulzana's Raid draws its dialectic tension from basic elements essential to the Western genre itself, namely the merging of history, romantic myth and formulaic storytelling. Westerns, as Jim Kitses and John Cawelti have pointed out, are mythic American history.[1] Each time we participate in a cavalry charge, a stage holdup, a cattle stampede we relive the golden moment of the American past when civilization and frontier stood toe to toe, both with and against each other, formidable and equal. Within this moment we celebrate the archetypal American, moving easily between town and the wilderness, choosing patterns of conduct from an infinity of choices, living in an atmosphere of boundless freedom. To re-create over and over this romanticized American history on screen requires, quite obviously, immense shortcuts in exposition and development. Audiences are shown images that immediately suggest broad patterns of historical meaning. This is done through the Western story formula which employs the repeated use of familiar landscapes such as the Southwest desert-mountain country or the Wyoming grasslands, icons such as guns, horses, and barbed wire, and the use of stereotyped characters such as gunfighter heroes, ranchers' daughters and Indians.

George Fenin and William Everson, in *The Western: From Silents to Cinerama*, argue that Indians have been exploited in Westerns because one of the central appeals of the Western is fast action. Within this context "the main function of these Americans consisted in providing a convenient mass enemy and a series of spectacular moving targets."[2] Such a view, however, seems to ignore the traditional and necessary stereotypical function of all the characters in a Western. Anti-Indian racism does indeed exist in Western movies, but the problem is not one of vicious stereotyping but one of the romantic distortions of history for purposes of creating mythic narrative.

American historical progress has been portrayed in two main ways in Westerns. A majority of Westerns, as Nicholas Garnham puts it, "are generally optimistic portraits of a dream becoming reality, in which a theory of original goodness still outweighs the fact of original sin . . . . the physical frontier is still a reality, if only just, and as long as that frontier exists the sheer exhilaration of physical progress, if forward movement, compensates for all the failures, for all the violence against man and nature that went into the building of America."³ Westerns celebrate progress and settlement. If the Indians were part of the landscape that needed to be tamed, then to destroy them may be unfortunate, even tragic, but is allowable and necessary in the name of inevitable historical whiteman's progress. To stereotype Indians as treacherous, cunning, and sadistically violent is to make their defeat in these Westerns all the more symbolically satisfying. Great obstacles provide for great accomplishments.

A second type of Western takes the opposite perspective. The white settlement of the West is viewed as violent conquest and progress is not a grand inevitability but a heartless and cruel incursion. Within the context of these antiprogress Westerns Indian tribal life becomes stereotyped as nobly virtuous, a proper alternative to the vulgarities of white society. In *Broken Arrow* (1950), for example, the Apaches keep their promises while whites break theirs. In *Little Big Man* (1971), Jack Crabb divides his life between white and Cheyenne societies, with the Cheyenne invariably morally superior.

The Indians in antiprogress Westerns are stereotyped as much as in the proprogress Westerns for the same basic reason: they are used to maintain a symbolic white historical viewpoint. Indians have become virtuous to allow white audiences to suffer purgative guilt in their guilt-ridden past. At their most exploitative, antiprogress Westerns stereotype Indians for paternalism or pontification. In *Billy Jack* (1971), for example, the half-breed title character undergoes Indian initiation rituals but becomes truly admirable only after he adopts the philosophical pacifism of the white woman he loves. Billy is morally superior to the corrupt townspeople in the picture, but nonetheless a system of morality designed by white intellectuals ultimately carries the day. In *Soldier Blue* (1970), innocent Indians are slaughtered by the cavalry but all too obviously to point an accusing finger at the infamous My Lai massacre in Vietnam. Thus, proprogress Westerns may be criticized for stereotyping Indians as diabolical for white glorification, but the opposite approach of the antiprogress Westerns may be criticized just as severely for stereotyping Indians as saintly, an occasion for white historical breast-beating or, worse, white condescension.⁴

Ulzana's Raid opens with the flight of ten heavily armed Chiricahua Apaches from the San Carlos Indian reservation in Arizona. Aldrich pauses to catch the Apache leader in a medium closeup. We recognize immediately that we are in the world of the old Western. Ulzana (Joaquín Martínez) is inscrutable, as expected, and behind those wrinkled lines and those burning eyes we know there is fierceness, terror and cruelty. That face is hundreds of Westerns old, and there is no doubt that before this picture is over many men will die. Our location in the proprogress Western is confirmed when Aldrich cuts away to an establishing shot of Fort Lowell. The fort is mostly tents with a few tossed-together wooden buildings. In the vastness of the flat desert it appears weak and vulnerable. The convention tells us that Ulzana's destruction is assured, but the beginning odds favor him and the struggle will be a formidable one.

As we settle back in the security of the icons and stereotypes we have been at home with for so long, Aldrich suddenly switches conventions. The cavalrymen are playing baseball. Baseball existed in the 1880s but never in Westerns and the balls and strikes seem too modern for an old Western.[5] Our confusion increases a few minutes later when the cavalry officers, having heard of Ulzana's escape, coolly refuse to let cavalry outriders accompany settlers back to the fort because there have been no orders to do so. Military procedure taking precedence over common-sense humaneness is an antimilitary gesture typical of antiprogress Westerns.

Aldrich plays this game throughout *Ulzana's Raid*. Conventions of Westerns celebrating white progress are contrasted with conventions celebrating Indian traditions and showing the hypocrisy of white values. Thesis continually opposes antithesis.

Conventions of proprogress Westerns are most often employed in the action sequences of the film, including the last minute rescue by the cavalry at the picture's climax. Calvary scout McIntosh (Burt Lancaster) is easily identifiable as the hero. When an officer says he is "a willful opinionated man with a contempt for all authority," we recognize in the comment a heritage going back at least as far as Natty Bumppo. McIntosh, as expected, demonstrates his heroism in a traditional way. In a beautifully filmed tracking shot across a grassy plain, Lancaster pulls his Winchester at a full gallop, cocks, shoots, has his horse shot out from under him, and comes up Winchester blazing, all in one breathless, poetic motion.

The action cuts back and forth between the activities of the cavalry and those of the renegade Apaches. During the Apache sequences Aldrich's portrayal of the Indians is nearly fanatical. In one scene, Ulzana and his bunch hack out the heart of a trooper and play catch with it. Another of their victims is burned alive. A woman is raped into insanity.[6] Much of this is shown in explicit detail. Ulzana's activities are dramatized to such a degree that they approach parody. Through it all Ulzana himself remains impassive, planning his heinous crimes meticulously, never offering more than a tiny smile when some ghastly piece of mischief has gone successfully.

Between the film's action scenes, Aldrich inserts interludes of relative inaction during which the members of the cavalry discuss the implications of the carnage Ulzana has left in his path. During these conversations, true to the new Westerns, the Indians emerge as the civilized, the whites as the savages. Having witnessed one of Ulzana's mutilated victims young Lt. DeBuin (Bruce Davison) asks the Apache scout Ke-Ni-Tay (Jorge Luke) why his people are so cruel. "Each man that dies—the man who kills him takes his power," Ke-Ni-Tay explains. "Here in this land, man must have power. Ulzana is a long time in the Agency. His power is very thin." Ulzana's activities are thus consistent with his cultural and religious heritage and are therefore honorable. Those of the cavalry, however, become increasingly less so. Lt. DeBuin is horrified when he discovers troopers mutilating the body of Ulzana's slain son. Whites have no cultural justification for such behavior. Lest the audience miss the lesson, Aldrich has McIntosh make it explicit. "What bothers you, Lieutenant, is you don't like to think of white men behaving like Indians. Kind of confuses the issue, don't it?" But DeBuin himself begins to fall victim to his unconscious racial bigotry. His resentment of Ke-Ni-Tay becomes more apparent with each interlude and climaxes with his demand that Ke-Ni-Tay bury a man Ulzana has killed because, "Damn it, that used to be a white man." DeBuin's racism is ironically emphasized by Ke-Ni-Tay's obvious superiority over DeBuin as a soldier. DeBuin at one point, ignoring all advice, causes the senseless death of one of his troopers. Ke-Ni-Tay, on the other hand, forms part of the plan that eventually destroys Ulzana. A recurring situation in movies by Robert Aldrich, such as *Ten Seconds to Hell* (1958), *Attack* (1956), and *The Dirty Dozen* (1967), is "highly neurotic men living in an atmosphere of hysteria."[7] Aldrich's dialectic method of alternating proprogress Western conventions in action scenes and antithetical antiprogress Western conventions in dialogue scenes creates not only a sense of hysteria on the screen but also in the audience. With conflicting stereotypes each cancelling out the significance of the other, there would seem to be no signposts; one simply cannot find the way. There are signposts, however. Aldrich provides a synthesis of his dialectical opposites by symbolically uniting two neurotic men of opposite cultures, Lt. DeBuin and Ke-Ti-Tay.

Although they seem vastly different largely because of their skills (Lt. DeBuin can't even do a decent job of calling balls and strikes during the baseball game), the two young men share similar personal problems. Ke-Ni-Tay has left the Agency Apaches to work for the white soldiers. He is an outsider amongst the whites, distrusted by them. His only obvious friend is McIntosh. DeBuin is an Easterner, not yet well enough trained to assume command in the Arizona wilderness and is distrusted by the enlisted men for being insecure and indecisive. The only man with any willingness to help DeBuin is McIntosh.

Most importantly, a similarity between the two is established through a mutually shared neurosis. Both men suffer from father fixations. Lt. DeBuin has volunteered for duty in the West to prove a theory of his minister-father's that it is "possible to be both a Christian and a soldier." He is given his first command, the job of bringing in Ulzana, because his commanding officer says it will give him a chance to test his father's theories. But DeBuin becomes an increasingly ineffective leader, as the chase progresses, and the harsh lessons of the landscape clash with the code his father has instilled in him. During one interlude, catching McIntosh reading the Bible, DeBuin interrupts to discuss how he hates Apaches; yet during another interlude, this time reading a Bible given to him by his father, DeBuin tells the Sergeant, "I wish I could ask him [his father] about the Apache. . . . the Apache was made in God's image like ourselves." DeBuin cannot lead effectively until the last moments of the picture when he considers allowing the mortally wounded McIntosh to die where he is instead of dragging him back to the fort. "But it's not Christian," DeBuin says. "That's right, Lieutenant, it's not," replies McIntosh. DeBuin decides to honor McIntosh's request thereby choosing to ignore the Eastern precepts of his father in favor of a more humane action growing from his experiences in combat. DeBuin completes his rejection of his past by ignoring the orders of the fort commanders (who had given him his command in the name of his father) to bring in the body of

Ulzana and allows Ke-Ni-Tay to bury the dead warrior according to Apache custom.

The source of Ke-Ni-Tay's neurosis is hidden somewhere in the past. One brief scene, however, provides a clue as to why he would leave his own people to live a lonely, isolated life with whites. Ke-Ni-Tay tells the troopers that Ulzana's wife and his wife are sisters. Then Ke-Ni-Tay adds, with almost comic casualness, "His wife ugly. My wife not so ugly." It is Ke-Ni-Tay's only real moment of apparent conversation—he otherwise speaks in the film only to convey important information or offer advice. His seemingly idle comment suggests a moment of dramatic revelation about his past. Ulzana as an old, seasoned warrior would be an object of great respect to a young warrior like Ke-Ni-Tay. Yet Ke-Ni-Tay slightly hints that Ulzana committed adultery with Ke-Ni-Tay's wife, an act against all Apache domestic codes, and a crime against the pride and dignity of Ke-Ni-Tay. Like DeBuin, Ke-Ni-Tay also puts aside the tarnished father figure at the end of the film. Ke-Ni-Tay hunts down Ulzana and, in a ritualistic ceremony of death, kills him. This done, Ke-Ni-Tay regains his Apache identity. He insists that Ulzana's body be left in his care, to be buried according to tribal custom.

In the midst of the ideological and psychological strugglings raging throughout the film, McIntosh is like the still point in a hurricane. Burt Lancaster nicely underplays his role. McIntosh rarely yells, never gets excited. McIntosh is personally at peace. A skillful Indian fighter, McIntosh still enjoys reading the Bible. A defender of the white settlers, McIntosh has an Apache wife. There is no sense in hating the Indians, McIntosh tells DeBuin. It would "be like hating the desert cuz there ain't no water on it." McIntosh has no need to bend his perspective of the wilderness to fit the needs of a preconceived ideal as does DeBuin and, to a lesser extent, Ke-Ni-Tay. McIntosh, in refusing to hate, quietly accepts both the whites and the Indians. "Hell," he says, "ain't none of us right." He lives accordingly, choosing freely from what he admires most about both cultures.

While DeBuin and Ke-Ni-Tay spend most of the film disposing of their old father figures, each gradually accepts McIntosh as a new father image. DeBuin begins by being suspicious of the independent McIntosh but puts increasing confidence in him and by the end of the picture relies on his advice entirely. Ke-Ni-Tay and

McIntosh are close friends from the moment the search for Ulzana begins. In the final scenes they grasp each other's arms in a father-son-like embrace.

The Christian platitudes of DeBuin's father represent the weakness of the antiprogress Western, an oversimplified view of morality with a tendency to exploit Indians for the sake of salvaging white self-righteousness in the face of the evidence of white evil. Ulzana's murderous rampage typifies the Indian stereotypes of the proprogress Western. Both DeBuin and Ke-Ni-Tay are therefore suffering from the two romantic distortions of history present in nearly all Westerns. Their rejection of the thesis and antithesis of past Westerns and their adoption of McIntosh as a new father offers the symbolic possibility to the Western of a synthesis of historical perspective, a synthesis in which "ain't none of us right" and the treatment of the Indians on the screen will cease to be exploitative.

Unfortunately, the possibilities of a further evolution in the Western suggested by *Ulzana's Raid* was not realized in later 1970s films. Robert Aldrich continued the theme of subcultural conflict in pictures he directed after *Ulzana's Raid*. *Emperor Of The North* (1973) pits freedom-loving hobos against sadistic railroad goons during the 1930s. *The Longest Yard* (1974) is centered around a symbolic football game in which the opponents are prisoners and prison guards. But Aldrich has made no other Westerns. Also, since 1972, no major American Western film has dealt with Indian-white conflict. It is almost as if *Ulzana's Raid* so completely exposed the major conventions of the past that traditional Indian-cavalry pictures are no longer appropriate, whereas new directions in the form suggested by *Ulzana's Raid* but never clearly outlined must await fresh, innovative creators of Westerns.

Ulzana's Raid, in both its basic storyline and in its rugged action sequences, is an exciting, exhilarating Western. At the same time its dialectical structure makes the movie important to the history of Western films in that the structure is itself a comment on the Western form. By revealing the deficiencies in both types of traditional Westerns, and by being itself a successful Western while eschewing those stereotypes, *Ulzana's Raid* demonstrates the vitality of the Western genre. Even though a new mythic concept of the frontier Indian-white wars has not been presented in Westerns through the late 1970s, *Ulzana's Raid* in 1972 at least demonstrated that such a new mythic perception could indeed be contained within the conventions and traditions of the Western movie form.

NOTES

1. Jim Kitses, *Horizons West* (Bloomington and London: Indiana University Press, 1969); John G. Cawelti, *The Six-Gun Mystique* (Bowling Green: Bowling Green Popular Press, 1971).

2. George N. Fenin and William K. Everson, *The Western: From Silents to Cinerama* (New York: Bonanza Books, 1962), p. 39.

3. Nicholas Garnham, *Samuel Fuller* (New York: Viking Press, 1971), p. 121.

4. White condescension, although more prevalent in the Western since 1950, is by no means an exclusively modern tendency in Westerns. In *The Vanishing American* (1925), for example, Richard Dix plays a Navaho who undergoes an identity crisis until he discovers the wisdom of the Bible.

5. An interesting note on baseball appears in Philip French, *Westerns* (New York: Oxford University Press, 1977), pp. 180–81.

6. Aldrich is so intent on dramatizing Ulzana's rampage as stereotyped that he apparently ignored cultural accuracy. According to one study, Chiricahua Apache were traditionally reticent in sexual matters. The raping of women when on raids was looked upon by the Chiricahua with extreme disfavor and it rarely took place. See Morris Edward Opler, *An Apache Life-Way: The Economic, Social and Religious Institutions of the Chiricahua Indians* (Chicago: University of Chicago Press, 1941), p. 351.

7. Ian Jarvie, "Hysteria and Authoritarianism in the Films of Robert Aldrich," *Film Culture* 22 (1961):104.

13

THE MISSOURI BREAKS (1976)

Floyd B. Lawrence

Floyd B. Lawrence is professor of English at Edinboro State College, Edinboro, Pennsylvania.

The Missouri Breaks, written by Thomas McGuane and directed by Arthur Penn, is a film of mythic dimensions that coherently reveals what scholars of myth loosely call the "monomyth" that underlies all specific pagan or Christian manifestations. Although the mythic hero I detect in the film is a variation of the vegetation god, it would be futile to search for an Orpheus, a Dionysos, an Osiris, or a Christ in Penn's Montana Badlands. But it is especially fruitful to seek for the common qualities of these and other mythic figures in *The Missouri Breaks.*

Perhaps the most obvious clue to the filmmakers' intentions is found in the three references to David Braxton's (John McLiam) resemblance to God, which are spoken early in the film by Little Tod (Randy Quaid). "That's old man Braxton," Tod whispers during the trial in the saloon, "Don't he look like God?" Indeed, not only does Braxton *look* like God; the film's structure leaves no doubt that he *is* God, and that the cycle of divine rise and fall provides a framework for the film's plot.

As the credits roll at the opening, we watch Braxton and two of his retainers approach on horseback through a lush valley of high grass. The present king of vegetation is heard as he reminisces

Floyd B. Lawrence, "The Mythic Waters of *The Missouri Breaks,*" *Journal of Popular Film* 5 no. 2 (1976). © 1976 by *The Journal of Popular Film.* Reprinted by permission of the publisher.

about the past glories of his land. But all is not well in his kingdom. The abruptly inserted hanging scene, excessively ugly in its visual impact, offers one proof of this unsettled state. But an even subtler note of tenuousness appears in the foreground of the scene as Braxton and his men ride in from the distance. In the foreground in sharp focus is a clump of dandelions gone to seed, a visual metaphor of transience *and* the possibility of new growth.

We are hardly prepared to accept Tom Logan (Jack Nicholson) as the seed of that growth when we first meet him: a boyish prankster, lamenting the death of Sandy, the hanged rustler, but eager to ride off to a Buster Keatonish train robbery and the local brothel. In view of his later functions, however, Logan is what every mythic protagonist is in his preheroic state, unconscious of the serious mission which awaits him and filled with no more than immediate intentions to exploit Braxton. Moreover, he is leading an "underground" existence, sporting good-naturedly with friends who implicitly acknowledge his role as leader. With his dispossessed family background, he is even more qualified for the task that lies ahead, the task of renewing that which has irretrievably decayed during the (brackish) Braxton reign.

Braxton's decadence surrounds him: in the "eight thousand Texas half-bred cattle and thirty-five hundred volumes of English literature in my library" (he reads the Neo-Classical *Tristram Shandy*, a book whose compassionate playfulness is crudely parodied by Braxton's bored and inhuman playing during the saloon trial scene), in the departed wife (who has, we are told, run off "with the first unreasonable man she could find," a description appropriate to Logan himself), and in a rebellious daughter (whose ritualized deflowering by Logan makes her the link between the old god and the new). A lonely Olympian from the Golden Age—he boasts of being in the California gold-fields before he was eighteen—with only a waning power for solace, Braxton uses language that reflects his counting-house sense of values. Being is quantified in all of his dealings, and his quantities are rapidly diminishing.

Little wonder, then, that he calls in the "regulator," Robert E. Lee Clayton (Marlon Brando), in a desperate and misdirected attempt to arrest things, to reestablish the status quo. The stage for the major conflict is set. Clayton is the scornful agent of a static old world of inhuman values, a grotesque version of his Virginia warrior namesake: Logan the innocent initiate whose actions will usher in a new world of growth and sensitivity.

Appropriately, Clayton's weapon is an elegantly tooled but deadly Creedmore rifle, a phallus of detached destruction. His victims are spied through the distorting lenses of a pair of binoculars. Even Clayton's affinity for birds brings to mind the bird dispatched by Zeus for the daily torment of the rebel Prometheus. Clayton's sadistic and inventive delight in eliminating the rustlers is no less horrendous. What is more, the moments at which Logan's three friends are killed are portentous: one is killed while defecating, another during coitus, and a third while asleep. The common element is the analogous condition of vulnerability, mortality, and privacy associated with all three occasions. Clayton's choice of those moments confirms not his inhumanity but his militantly anti-human state of mind. Even his name suggests the elemental clay to which his nihilistic vision would reduce all being.

Clayton's disguises—as a Buffalo-Bill type in resplendent buckskins, as a clergyman, as an old lady—reveal even more about his function. As a variously-clad and many-accented cynic with no real allegiances except to the act of "regulation" itself, Clayton may be taken as a perverse Everyman, a Satanic incarnation of the people, the countries, and the institutions that stand in fanatical defense of the old god. Despite Brando's own attempts at making his role into something mythic in itself, McGuane's description of Clayton in the screenplay makes the writer's intention fairly clear: "He looks like an early day Methodist itinerant proselytizer." Clayton reminds one of the character dressed in patchwork in Joseph Conrad's *Heart of Darkness*, who mindlessly follows the god-like but demented Kurtz; Conrad's narrator describes him in terms that would be broadly appropriate for Clayton: "Then he was before me, in motley, as though he had absconded from a troupe of mimes, enthusiastic, fabulous, His very existence was improbable, inexplicable, and altogether bewildering." And, like Kurtz, Clayton is a hollow man, little more than a voice or voices with shifting identities. "He never seems to be quite there," McGuane writes of him in the screenplay.

Logan, on the other hand, with the assistance of the virgin daughter of the old god, renews the land instinctively, recognizing it as the source of the dynamic future rather than the static present. His place in the cultural cycle is spelled out by the rancher (James Greene) to whom Cary (Frederic Forrest) sells horses: "Ole Thomas Jefferson said he was a warrior so his son could be a farmer so *his* son could be a poet." No hint is given of the poet who will presumably displace Logan one day, although Logan himself is seen briefly as the artist type when he tries to play a clarinet he has acquired in trade for horses. The time for music has not arrived, but the time of the farmer, historically and mythically, is here. The warrior mentality of Braxton and Clayton faces imminent extinction. When the cynical Calvin (Harry Dean Stanton) becomes short-tempered with the changed Logan and insists on knowing just what the rustler turned sodbuster is about, Logan responds: "Well, Calvin, I'm just . . . trying to make it look like a real ranch, you know, a . . . real place where people are living." This is as close as Logan comes to articulating a conscious awareness of his destined role.

Initially, Logan is reluctant to remain at the ranch while his three friends go into Canada for more horses. (Mercifully, the extended encounter between these three and the tracking Mounties that is written into the screenplay is abbreviated in the film; we receive the dominant impression, through shots of the racing horses, of confined spirits being freed from military ownership, but the episode remains largely irrelevant to the mythic goings-on.) When Jane Braxton (Kathleen Lloyd) later visits Logan at the ranch, he exhibits a modest pride in his pastoral accomplishments. He directs her to lift a board that releases the irrigating waters into the garden. The camera lingers on this action of symbolic renewal. "I admire you," Jane says, to which Logan replies, "That's the whole idea, lady." Logan's role as the bearer of the new logos, the word of life, is firmly established. Also established is the pervasive significance of images of water throughout the film, an image which is introduced in the screenplay as early as the opening scene description: "Northern Montana in the early 1880s: A vast grassland where cloud shadows move as though it were the sea."

In each of the three fateful Logan-Clayton encounters, water functions to remind the viewer of the symbolic dimension of the conflict. After taunting Logan during the first encounter in the garden (in the screenplay, Logan is "attending the birth of a foal" when the regulator appears), Clayton gleefully shoots at heads of cabbages and lettuce, ostensibly to intimidate Logan but actually to continue in his role as denier of life on even the most elemental levels. In a bit of his own taunting, Logan asks Clayton: "Did you ever hit a guy from a mile off while he was carrying a pail of water?"

The second encounter, the seemingly inscrutable bathtub scene, makes perfect sense if the significance of water is allowed. Here Clayton is immersed not in water so much as in a decadent—it *is* a tub fashioned by Braxton for his departed wife—bubble-bath reduction of water. (The association of water, death, and Clayton has been made earlier when Clayton rudely picks a corpse up from its coffin in Braxton's living room, scattering ice from the coffin around the room. And later Clayton drowns Little Tod under the guise of teaching him how to cross the river on horseback. The latter scene, shot from the perspective of the drowning man, brings Clayton's menace home to the viewer in frightening terms: as we watch Clayton through the liquid medium, we have a first-hand sense of the subversion of the powers of water, from life-giving to life-taking.) Although Logan cannot kill the bathing Clayton, he does use his gun as an irrigation tool of sorts. Firing into the tub, he releases the waters which are there—even if the hollow Clayton "isn't there"—and which run downstairs, dripping from Braxton's chandlier, dousing the lights of Braxton's shrunken cosmos. That the chandelier may be taken symbolically is, incidentally later justified when Braxton angrily stands up and bumps his head on it, a joking piece of anthromorphism equal to any.

The third encounter, the throat-slitting, has little obvious reference to the water motifs of the preceding scenes. Obliquely, however, a connection can be made. After wooing and serenading his horse, actions which the horse denies in its urinary response (that humorously but undeniably continues the natural process of fertilizing the earth), Clayton retires for the night. "Old Granny's tired," he sighs as he settles in. Indeed, the "old granny," the old earth mother that Logan must reawaken, is tired, dried up, no longer possessed of physical or spiritual nourishment. Clayton is ironically correct, and his death only confirms how tired granny really is. Clayton's perverse relationship to cosmic nature is caught also when, shortly before killing Calvin, he coyly refers to the Star of Bethlehem, claiming he can almost see it if he looks the right way. And the screenplay contains this pertinent description of Clayton's pathetic sense of a lost something: "Lee Clayton riding toward a stirring, immense sky. He studies the beautiful clouds and the shafts of imperial light. He smiles into the effulgence of nature and his eyes fill with tears." As portrayed by Brando, the character of Lee Clayton is not a tearful one; Brando's Clayton, nevertheless, is a man whose end is imminent.

The murder of Clayton is preceded by a momentous sequence in the career of Logan as young god. Like so many heroes of myth, Logan must either die or descend to an underworld experience (or both). Of course, Penn cannot employ the magic of literal death and resurrection in a genre film employing the verisimilitude of the stock Western. But he can and he does suggest this mythic motif during the interlude when Logan discovers the deaths of his three close friends. Significantly, one of those friends, Si (John Ryan), is gunned down by Clayton at a ranch called Hellsgate. Especially rich in implication, in fact the nadir of Logan's descent into a realization of mortality, is Logan's gruesome chance confrontation with Cary's corpse. As Logan stares at the blue-gray body propped up in a vertical coffin, resembling a hideous fetus with its tilted head and crossed arms tied into place, the hastily lettered sign above the coffin shocks with its resonance: "Do you know this man?" Of course Logan knows this man, but Logan's real knowledge is of the mortality that the hero must recognize in his journey from innocence to experience. Only with the disturbing knowledge of mortality can he qualify as a seeker after immortality. Later, after the execution of Clayton, the blank screen captures the precise moment of Logan's descent into the black Hades of death.

With the militant forces of the old god now out of the way, the final violent and purgative encounter (and such encounters, myth after myth tells us, *must* be violent) can occur. Returning to the Braxton ranch, Logan finds Jane, dressed appropriately but prematurely in black, and the dying, half-mad father, served by a single retainer whose futile but devoted care for Braxton provides an ironic counterpoint to Clayton's "service." Logan desires only the daughter, but he is forced into violent response. The shooting of the old man, however, is but a variation of Logan's earlier "enabling" shot into the bathtub. Like Clayton, the dying old god "isn't there" in any essential way. Of great figurative import is Logan's act of throwing the ornate Creedmore rifle through the window, a bursting through the suffocating confines of Braxton's kingdom and a violent parallel to the gentle deflowering of Braxton's daughter. As lover *and* as (reluctant) warrior, Logan thereby succeeds in completing the transition from old to new, from sterility to the possibility of fertility.

It is of some interest to note that the published screenplay contains a quite different conclusion which nevertheless does not alter the conclusions about Tom Logan that I have reached in this discussion. McGuane constructs a scene that brings Tom back to the Braxton ranch, engages him in a brief dual with Braxton, and shows him leading Jane into the master bedroom. Different as this action is from that which appears in the film, it merely confirms, albeit in a different fashion, the replacement of Braxton's prerogatives by Logan's own.

The very last scene in the film, a cautious but not unduly pessimistic coda, portrays Logan shyly but confidently arranging for a tentative future liaison with Miss Braxton. Firmly established is Logan's intention to go north, to some vaguely defined locale "where the waters run all year." That line, together with the film's title, suggesting a critical juncture in the Heraclitean flux, undeniably asserts the overriding importance of water as iterative image and the subsequent reality of the vegetation god myth as the basis of the film's symbolic plot. The irresolution of Logan's immediate aims may stem from the absence of any broad communal context that normally surrounds such a hero (although the film audience itself, as versed in generic conventions as the audience of Sophoclean tragedy, may provide a modern version of that context). Most striking of all, perhaps, is that the film performs its metonymic function neither overtly nor ostentatiously. The most authentic myths, after all, evolve like dreams, from mysteriously unspecified sources and give the semblance of unwilled individual and cultural process. If *The Missouri Breaks* is genre Western, it is nonetheless valid, if soft-spoken, universal myth.

Selected Bibliography

The following is a brief bibliography of books about Western movies. For a much more thorough listing of materials bearing on that topic, the reader should consult Jack Nachbar's *Western Films: An Annotated Critical Bibliography* (New York: Garland Publishing Company, 1975).

Bazin, André. *What Is Cinema?* Vol. 2. Translated by Hugh Gray. Berkeley: University of California Press, 1971. Reprints three of Bazin's historically important essays on Westerns: "The Western, or the American Film par Excellence," "The Evolution of the Western," and *"The Outlaw."*

Cawelti, John G. *The Six-Gun Mystique.* Bowling Green, Ohio: Popular Press, 1971. An indispensable work. Brings together the author's ideas, developed earlier in a series of journal articles, on the character and plot formulas most often associated with the "Western myth." Contains a list of major Western films and directors. Cawelti's *Adventure, Mystery, and Romance* (Chicago: University of Chicago Press, 1976) includes a lengthy chapter on Westerns that further elaborates his concepts.

Eyles, Allen. *The Western: An Illustrated Guide.* New York: A. S. Barnes and Company, 1967. Useful reference work, containing biographical data on actors, scriptwriters, directors, cameramen, and others involved in making Westerns. Brief bibliography.

Fenin, George N., and William K. Everson. *The Western: From Silents to the Seventies.* New York: Grossman Publishers, 1973. Updates the authors' *The Western: From Silents to Cinerama,* published in 1962. Fenin and Everson consistently invoke "realism" as their standard for judging Western films. Despite the simplicity of this critical approach, *The Western* is an invaluable source of information on the historical development of the genre.

French, Philip. *Westerns: Aspects of a Movie Genre.* Revised Edition. New York: Oxford University Press, 1977. A witty and reliable discussion of Westerns as a movie type. Highly recommended.

Kitses, Jim. *Horizons West.* Bloomington: Indiana University Press, 1969. Offers, in its opening chapter, an excellent structural analysis of the Western genre. The remainder of the work is a detailed exploration of the films of three leading directors of Westerns—Anthony Mann, Budd Boetticher, and Sam Peckinpah.

Manchel, Frank. *Cameras West.* Englewood Cliffs, New Jersey: Prentice-Hall, 1971. Apparently written for a high-school-age audience. Readable and informative. Especially good on the silent period.

Nachbar, Jack, ed. *Focus on the Western.* Englewood Cliffs, New Jersey: Prentice-Hall, 1974. Collects fifteen essays and articles that provide illuminating overviews of the Western. Helpful chronology and bibliography.

Parish, James Robert, and Michael R. Pitts. *The Great Western Pictures.* Metuchen, New Jersey: Scarecrow Press, 1976. Quirky and uneven. Supplies, nevertheless, much useful information on several hundred alphabetically listed Westerns: production details, plot summaries, quotes from reviews.

Parkinson, Michael, and Clyde Jeavons. *A Pictorial History of Westerns.* London: Hamlyn, 1972. Important primarily, as the title suggests, for the pictorial glimpses it affords of the Western's chronological development. "The Films," "The Stars," and "The Directors" are sample chapter headings.

Silver, Charles. *The Western Film.* New York: Pyramid Productions, 1976. Brief, highly opinionated survey from the silents to the present. Silver adores the "classical Western" (his term) and eschews those films that rebel against its tradition. A generous number of stills, short bibliography and filmography.

Tuska, Jon. *The Filming of the West.* Garden City, New York: Doubleday, 1976. A breezy, chatty history of Western films. The book's most useful service is that it records much indispensable biographical and production data relating to the makers and the making of about one hundred important Western movies. Excellent array of still photographs.

Wright, Will. *Sixguns and Society: A Structural Study of the Western.* Berkeley: University of California Press, 1975. A sometimes pretentious, but ultimately very helpful examination of Westerns from a structuralist vantage point.